World Wisdom
The Library of Perennial Philosophy

The Library of Perennial Philosophy is dedicated to the exposition of the timeless Truth underlying the diverse religions. This Truth, often referred to as the *Sophia Perennis*—or Perennial Wisdom—finds its expression in the revealed Scriptures as well as in the writings of the great sages and the artistic creations of the traditional worlds.

The Essential Śrī Ānandamayī Mā: Life and Teachings of a 20th Century Indian Saint appears as one of our selections in the Spiritual Masters: East & West series.

Spiritual Masters: East & West Series

This series presents the writings of great spiritual masters of the past and present from both East and West. Carefully selected essential writings of these sages are combined with biographical information, glossaries of technical terms, and pictorial and photographic art in order to communicate a sense of their respective spiritual climates.

The Essential Śrī Ānandamayī Mā

Life and Teachings of a 20th Century Indian Saint

Biography by
Alexander Lipski

Words of
Śrī Ānandamayī Mā
translated by Ātmānanda

Edited by
Joseph A. Fitzgerald

World Wisdom

*The Essential Śrī Ānandamayī Mā: Life and Teachings
of a 20th Century Indian Saint*

Life and Teaching of Anandamayi Ma by Alexander Lipski; © Motilal Banarsidass Publishers Pvt Ltd.
41 UA Bungalow Road, Jawahar Nagar, Delhi-110007; www.mlbd.com
Words of Anandamayi Ma; translated and compiled by Atmananda. Courtesy of the Shree Shree
Anandamayee Sangha; Head Office, Kankhal, Hardwar, 249408

Photographs on pp. *xi*, 22, 31, 32, 33, 41, 73, 102, 103, and 108 © Richard Lannoy from
Anandamayi: Her Life and Wisdom

Book design by Susana Marín

Library of Congress Cataloging-in-Publication Data

Lipski, Alexander, 1919-
  The essential Sri Anandamayi Ma : life and teachings of a 20th century Indian saint / biography
by Alexander Lipski ; words of Sri Anandamayi Ma translated by Atmananda ; edited by Joseph A.
Fitzgerald.
     p. cm. — (The library of perennial philosophy. Spiritual masters—East & West series)
  Includes translations from Bengali.
  Includes bibliographical references and index.
  ISBN 978-1-933316-41-3 (pbk. : alk. paper) 1. Anandamayi, 1896-1982. 2. Hindu women saints-
-Biography. I. Anandamayi, 1896-1982. Selections. English. 2007. II. Fitzgerald, Joseph A., 1977- III.
Title.
  BL1175.A49L57 2007
  294.5092—dc22
  [B]

                                                                                        2007018087

Printed on acid-free paper in China.

For information address World Wisdom, Inc.
P.O. Box 2682, Bloomington, Indiana 47402-2682
www.worldwisdom.com

Contents

Preface

We wish to express our thanks to those custodians of Mā's spiritual legacy, the Shree Shree Anandamayee Sangha, as well as to Motilal Banarsidass Publishers, for allowing us to produce the present work, in which two important books are edited[1] and combined into a single account of the life and teachings of the great twentieth century saint of India, Śrī Ānandamayī Mā (1896-1982), the bliss-permeated Mother.

In his book *Life and Teaching of Śrī Ānandamayī Mā*, published by Motilal Banarsidass, Professor Alexander Lipski offers us an engaging, concise, and spiritually sensitive biography of Ānandamayī Mā that is based on both thorough research and personal contact. Professor Lipski further provides us with an insightful interpretation of the significance of Ānandamayī Mā's personality and teaching. An edited rendering of Professor Lipski's writings on Ānandamayī Mā begins the present volume, forming the first and second chapters. No work on Ānandamayī Mā would, however, be complete without the inclusion of her actual words. To that end, the third and largest chapter of the present volume provides edited selections from Mā's discourses, recorded by Brahmacāri Kamal Bhattacharjee, and later translated into English by Ātmānanda, both close devotees. These discourses were published by the Shree Shree Anandamayee Sangha under the title *Words of Sri Anandamayi Ma*. We believe that, together, the biography by Professor Lipski along with the actual words of Ānandamayī Mā creates as complete a verbal representation as is possible of a woman who was herself beyond the level of duality, and thus, ultimately, beyond all description.

Anyone who was fortunate enough to meet Ānandamayī Mā—and there are many fortunate ones still living—knows that something of her teaching is in her very person. Thus we have chosen to illustrate this volume with photographs taken of Ānandamayī Mā over the course of her life, from youth to old age. We are especially grateful to Richard Lannoy for allowing us the use of his incomparable photographs taken in Mā's later years. It is said that one receives a blessing of presence through the *darśana* (literally "sight") of a saint: May the bliss-permeated Mother bless us by her presence!

Joseph A. Fitzgerald

---

[1] General editorial changes made include: deletion of certain passages; re-ordering of certain passages; harmonization of spelling conventions; addition of certain footnotes and intertextual notes; and replacement of certain Sanskrit terms by their English translation. In order to facilitate readability, we have not noted deletions or alterations within the text.

Alexander Lipski (b. 1919) was a Professor of History and Religious Studies at California State University from 1958 to 1984. He has been a Professor Emeritus from 1984 to the present.

Introduction

"Just imagine that a tree—a beautiful, strong, old beech for instance approaches you with calm steps. What would you feel? 'Have I gone crazy,' you would ask yourself. 'Or perhaps I am dreaming?' Finally you would have to concede that you had entered a new dimension of reality of which you had hitherto been ignorant." Thus the German novelist Melita Maschmann sums up her first impressions of Ānandamayī Mā (bliss-permeated Mother).

There is no question that Ānandamayī Mā is a spiritual giant who rightfully takes Her place among the great saints of modern India, such as Ramakrishna, Vivekananda, Aurobindo Ghose, Ramana Maharshi, and Paramahansa Yogananda. Her life is an eloquent testimony to the abiding strength of Indian spirituality. Her message is particularly appropriate in a world where the notion of progress is no longer taken for gospel truth and the whole array of our "modern values" is undergoing an agonizing reappraisal. Ānandamayī Mā diagnoses the present disease of civilization as "over-secularization." She suggests that the cure from our severe illness cannot be brought about by engineers, sociologists, or psychologists but by doctors of the soul. She prescribes a drastic revolution in our views and attitudes from outwardness to inwardness, from materialism to spirituality, and from man-centeredness to God-centeredness. Her totally uncompromising transcendent point of view is truly a shock therapy for problem-solving oriented, pragmatic Americans. She shows no apparent concern for the population explosion, environmental pollution, racism, political tensions, economic crises. And yet, as one of Her disciples expressed it, the purpose of Her being is "… to demonstrate the existence of a power that is ever at work creating by Its transforming influence, beauty out of ugliness, love out of strife. Such a power is Śrī Ānandamayī Mā. May She bring peace and harmony into this world of strife."

I first got interested in Ānandamayī Mā while reading about Her in Paramahansa Yogananda's *Autobiography of a Yogi*. Subsequently, I met several Americans who had visited Ānandamayī Mā for extended periods of time. In 1965, while spending my sabbatical leave in India, I visited Her *āśram*[1] in Vārāṇasi and then stayed with Ānandamayī Mā in Rajgir, the capital of an ancient Indian state. When I was brought into the presence of Ānandamayī Mā I felt that, for the first time in my life, I was encountering someone who was the very embodiment of the Holy, the "wholly other." And yet Ānandamayī Mā was also so close and accessible. She immediately welcomed me with a loving smile signifying total acceptance. In Her simple, unaffected way She asked me about my family and with genuine interest looked at the photos of my wife and my three daughters. She then gave me the privilege of sitting near Her. During the ensuing *satsaṅga*[2] I had an opportunity to observe Her at close quarters. I was struck by the youthful almost girlish appearance of the then sixty-nine year old Ānandamayī Mā. It was a delight to listen to Her pearly laughter, and I was struck by the ease and assurance with which the almost illiterate Ānandamayī Mā responded to the most recondite questions of erudite scholars. A highlight of my stay with Ānandamayī Mā was my personal interview during which I was alone with Her except for the presence of an interpreter. Facing Mātājī[3] I felt as though I was mentally stripped naked. It seemed to me that She could see into the innermost recesses of my mind. I asked Her to tell me what the chief obstacles on my spiritual path were. In re-

[1] Hermitage; a place where seekers after Truth live together under the guidance of a spiritual master.

[2] Literally "fellowship with truth." The company of saints, sages, and seekers after Truth. Religious meeting.

[3] Ānandamayī Mā is commonly addressed as "Mātājī" or "Mā," which are the Hindi and Bengali words for "mother."

sponse She revealed to me some glaring shortcomings of which I had been hitherto totally unaware. What She said was in no way flattering, in fact painful, but Ānandamayī Mā said it so compassionately, although firmly, that I did not feel condemned. I realized what true loving detachment was.

The days at Ānandamayī Mā's *āśram* flew by. Throughout my stay I had a feeling of utter contentment and peace—worldly problems were temporarily eclipsed. As though in the presence of a gigantic spiritual magnet my mind was engrossed in the Divine. When thinking of the blissful experiences in Rajgir, there flashes even now through my mind a scene of a *kīrtana*[4] with Mātājī. And I hear Her chanting "*He Bhagavān*" (Oh, Lord) to the accompaniment of a harmonium. Her chanting is the very expression of divine love and ecstasy and prompts me to echo the words of the Persian inscription on the Diwan-i-Khās:[5]

> If on Earth be an Eden of bliss
> it is this, it is this, none but this.

While I had a limited knowledge of Hindi at the time of my visit to Ānandamayī Mā I decided then and there to take up the study of Bengali, to be able to become acquainted in depth with the life and teaching of Mātājī. Through the kind assistance of Mr. K. Bose, Secretary of Shree Shree Anandamayee Sangha,[6] I was able to procure most of the literature in Bengali and English dealing with Ānandamayī Mā. The more I immersed myself in the life and thought of the bliss-permeated Mother, the clearer it became to me that many people in the west could profit from Her wisdom. When I discussed Ānandamayī Mā during my lectures on modern Hindu religious thought I was impressed by the enthusiastic response of the students who eagerly asked for more information about the bliss-permeated Mother. This prompted me to undertake the present study. Writing on the life and teaching of Ānandamayī Mā was a privilege in itself, but I am filled with gladness at the thought that through this study Mātājī will become better known and that many spiritual seekers who have become aware of the emptiness of a mere materialistic existence will find renewed meaningfulness.

Alexander Lipski

[4] Chanting or singing of the names or glories of God, performed by one person or a group of people.

[5] Private Audience Hall within the Fatehpur Sikri palace complex.

[6] Administrative body dedicated to furthering Mā's teachings and overseeing her *āśram*s.

CHAPTER I
Play of Life

"Before I came on this earth, Father, 'I was the same.' As a little girl, 'I was the same.' I grew into womanhood, but still 'I was the same'.... Ever afterwards though the dance of creation changes around me in the hall of eternity, 'I shall be the same.'" These words were addressed by the bliss-permeated Mother to Paramahansa Yogananda when he visited Her in Calcutta in 1936. They constitute a challenge to any attempt to superimpose an evolutionary pattern upon Her life. Terms, such as growth, advancement, and maturation, as referring to the spiritual aspect of Her life are inapplicable. Yet unquestionably an analysis of Her outward activities shows distinct developmental phases. While according to the Hindu view of life, all manifestation is God's *līlā* (sport, play), the expression seems particularly fitting when dealing with events in the life of Ānandamayī Mā, for She frequently alludes to the fact that She is a detached onlooker, performing voluntarily a play in this delusive earthly theater, on a stage limited by time and space.

Ānandamayī Mā was born on April 30, 1896 in Kheorā, a tiny village in the interior of East Bengal (now Bangladesh). British impact was then hardly noticeable in that remote, largely Muslim-inhabited area. The house in which She was born was completely surrounded by Muslim dwellings. At that time, fortunately, harmonious relations existed between Muslims and Hindus. Outbreaks of communal violence—chronic occurrences in the twentieth century—were unknown. The majority of the Muslims were converts from low caste Hindus and had still retained traces of their Hindu practices. There were even quite a few devotees of Mother Kālī among the Muslims. Yet it cannot be denied that Hindu caste restrictions con-stituted an insurmountable barrier preventing a close contact between the two communities.

Ānandamayī Mā's parents were devout *vaiṣṇavas*[1] and strict followers of caste regulations. Her father, Bipin Bihārī Bhattācārya, came from a distinguished *brāhman*[2] family. Most of his time was taken up with religious practices. He especially loved to chant devotional songs. For long periods he would be absent from his home, joining *kīrtana* (musical devotion) parties or going on pilgrimages to sacred sites. Her mother, Moksadā Sundarī, counted many pandits among her ancestors. Her family proudly

---

[1] Worshipper of Viṣṇu, the preserver and sustainer of the universe.

[2] The highest Indian caste.

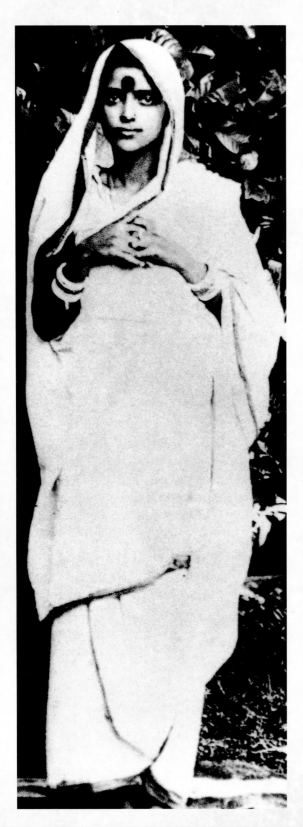

remembered that in the not too distant past one of their ancestors had joyously thrown herself on her dead husband's funeral pyre. Moksadā Sundarī shared her husband's fondness for spiritual chants. She even gained some reputation for composing devotional songs which are still popular among the village folk of her region.

Ānandamayī Mā was the second child, born three years after the first—also a daughter—had died at the age of nine months. It is reported that before the birth of Ānandamayī Mā Moksadā Sundarī had frequent dreams of gods and goddesses. At birth the future Ānandamayī Mā was given the name Nirmalā Sundarī (Immaculate Beauty). She grew up in an atmosphere of utmost simplicity bordering on penury, since Her father was not much of a provider, the growing family—four brothers and two sisters were born after Nirmalā—had to live from a small income derived from some minor landed property. Luckily Moksadā Sundarī was an exceedingly capable housewife who managed to work veritable miracles with her slender budget. But although Nirmalā never knew starvation, Her education was affected by the family's financial plight. She had to do Her school work on a broken slate because the parents could not afford to buy a new one. At times She could not be "spared" for school, since She had to help with the housework. Then again She missed school because no escort was available and She could not walk there alone. In total, Nirmalā attended school for less than two years. During that short period She impressed the teacher with Her sharp mind. Much later She reminisced: "Somehow or other, I invariably happened to look up the very questions the teacher would ask, and consequently he always found me well prepared even after long absences. The meaning of unknown words would occur to me spontaneously...." With less than two years of primary school to Her credit, Ānandamayī Mā can hardly be considered "educated." Although She is capable of writing[3] She normally auto-

[3] There is one specimen of Her writing (probably from

graphs books with a mere dot. When doing so, She sometimes remarks: "In this everything is contained." She never sees fit to read books, and thus just like the equally "uneducated" Ramakrishna Paramahansa,[4] testifies to the fact that wisdom is not dependent on book learning—a truth too shocking to be accepted by most academicians. The bliss-permeated Mother Herself once stated: "If someone really wants God, and nothing but God, he carries his book in his own heart. He needs no printed book."

From early childhood on Nirmalā exhibited a cheerful disposition, so that Her neighbors nicknamed Her *Hāsi Mā* (Mother of Smiles) or *Khusīr Mā* (Happy Mother). She felt equally at home among Hindus and Muslims. Her orthodox mother, naturally, insisted on safeguarding Nirmalā from contamination. Ritual purity had to be preserved: "As long as *annaprāśana* (ceremony when a baby first takes solid food at about five or six months) has not taken place, it is no sin to touch a Muslim. After that such contact requires an ablution." Many an ablution had to be administered to the Mother of Smiles! She also first met Christians while still a child. When Christian missionaries came to Kheorā and pitched a tent there, Nirmalā visited them and was greatly impressed by their sincerity and devoutness. She loved to listen to their hymn singing and begged Her mother to buy Her one of their Bengali hymn books. Many years later, in 1962, some German visitors sang Christian hymns to Ānandamayī Mā. She thoroughly enjoyed them and mentioned to the Germans that hearing the hymns reminded Her of Her childhood experience in Kheorā.

Nirmalā had no formal religious education. Normally in India children absorb religion by

1930). She wrote: "O thou Supreme Being, thou art manifest in all forms—this universe, with all created things, wife, husband, father, mother, and children, all in one. Man's mind is clouded by worldly ties. But there is no cause for despair. With purity, unflinching faith, and burning eagerness go ahead and you will realize your true Self." (Translation from Bengali)

[4] One of India's greatest modern saints, died 1886.

Nirmalā with her parents

from Her father and was soon seen joining him eagerly in daily worship. There were some early signs that the little Mother of Smiles was not an ordinary child, but the parents did not grasp their import. One day, for example, She casually asked Her mother: "Did not Mr. Nandan Cakravartī visit us shortly after I was born?" The mother was taken aback. It was true that a Mr. Cakravartī had called on them when Nirmalā was just a few days old, but they had never referred to his visit. How could Nirmalā possibly remember it? There were a few other instances suggesting that She must have been fully conscious of Her surroundings practically from the time of birth on. Also, once in a while She had spells of absentmindedness—obviously trances. Then again She was seen talking to plants and to apparently invisible beings. These instances were, however, rare, so that the parents were not unduly alarmed. Her cheerfulness and lovability more than compensated for Her occasional strange behavior. Her obedience was truly remarkable. Once a relative left Her in front of the local Śiva temple and told Her to remain there until her return. The relative became so involved in some errand that she forgot about Nirmalā. Many hours later, when she returned to the temple, she found the little girl sitting in the very position in which she had left Her.

As was customary at that time, a husband had to be found for the Mother of Smiles while She was still a child. The prospective husband

osmosis. They observe the adults and as soon as is feasible participate in *pūjā* (worship). Thus the little Nirmalā learnt devotional chanting

had to be of the proper caste, i.e., a *brāhman* and his family had to accept the fact that the dowry would be minimal. After a careful search the parents arranged for the marriage of Nirmalā to Ramani Mohan Cakravartī, later referred to as Bholānātha (a name for Śiva). He was the third son of Jagatbandhu Cakravartī and Tripura Sundari Devī who lived in Atpārā, a village in the district of Dacca. The marriage took place on February 7th, 1909, when Nirmalā was not quite thirteen years of age. While the age of Bholānāth is nowhere mentioned, it is known that he was considerably older than his wife. For the next five years the couple did not live together. Bholānāth, who had a very rudimentary education, was a clerk in the police depart-

ment at Atpārā at the time of marriage. After a few months he lost that job and for the next few years moved around all over East Bengal, finding temporary employment only. Until 1910 Nirmalā continued to live with Her parents. When She was fourteen years of age it seemed appropriate to send Her to Her husband's family, there to be prepared for Her future household duties. Ordinarily Her mother-in-law would have been in charge of Her. But, since Bholānāth's mother had died two years before his marriage, the function of training his wife devolved upon Pramodā Devī, the wife of his eldest brother, Revatī Mohan. This was in accordance with the hierarchical family order of India. In 1910, therefore, Nirmalā moved to

Nirmalā with
her husband
Bholānāth

Śrīpur, where Revatī Mohan's family lived. Both Revatī Mohan and Pramodā Devī became exceedingly fond of the little Mother of Smiles who adapted Herself easily to Her new environment, charming everyone with Her joyfulness. She took over practically all the household chores and soon excelled in spinning, needlework, weaving, and especially in cooking. She worked so hard at scrubbing pots and keeping the house clean that Her hands were covered with bruises. Many years later, when Her fame had already spread all over India, She met with Her sister-in-law, and the two exchanged happy reminiscences about village life in Śrīpur. Ānandamayī Mā acted completely naturally, as though She was still the young village girl. In front of a crowd of devotees, She said teasingly: "Look, all these housewives think that they are great experts in household work. Tell them whether I too did not look after your house satisfactorily?" Pramodā Devī eagerly assented to this. Indeed she had had reason to be greatly satisfied with her highly efficient and utterly obedient sister-in-law. The four years in Śrīpur were, at least outwardly, rather uneventful as far as Nirmalā's spiritual *līlā* is concerned. There were just a few instances of trances. Several times Pramodā Devī was attracted by the smell of burnt food to the kitchen, where she found Nirmalā unconscious on the kitchen floor. But Pramodā Devī was unsuspecting. She assumed that her hard working sister-in-law had fallen asleep from fatigue. Nirmalā's life in Śrīpur came to an end in 1913, a few months after Her brother-in-law Revatī Mohan had died. For about six months She stayed with Her parents. Then, in 1914, She joined Bholānāth in Astagrāma, also in East Bengal, where he had found employment in the Land Settlement Department. This was the actual beginning of their life together.

A most unusual marriage it was to be. So far Bholānāth had had no inkling of Nirmalā's extraordinary state. He had thought that he had married an ordinary village girl. He was slightly disappointed that She proved even less educated than he. At first he had sent Her books hoping to interest Her in improving Her reading but soon he realized that his wife had no scholarly inclinations. When he first tried to approach Her physically, he supposedly received such a violent electric shock that he put for the time being all thought of a physical re-lationship out of his mind. He seems to have initially thought that this was only a temporary condition, that Nirmalā was still such a child and that She would later become "normal." But the marriage was never physically consummated. As far as Nirmalā is concerned, the question of sexual desire did not even arise. In 1938, after Bholānāth's death, She told Didi:[5] "There never was any shadow of a worldly thought in Bholānāth's mind. He made no difference between me and little Maroni (his sister's granddaughter) when we lay near him at night. You will remember that many times when you were going away at night, you laid me down near him when this body[6] was in ecstasy. He was never

[5] Didi, Gurupriyā Devī, one of Her closest devotees.

[6] Ānandamayī Mā refers to Herself usually as "this body" or as "this little daughter of yours." She usually addresses all unmarried people as Her friends and married people as Her fathers or mothers.

troubled by any self-consciousness. In Bajītpur, as well as in Shah-bagh, he guarded and looked after this body most confidently and unselfconsciously. Once or twice, when there was an inkling of a worldly thought in him which was

so unformed as not to be on the level of his consciousness, this body would assume all the symptoms of death. He would feel frightened and do *japa* (repetition of a divine phrase or name) knowing that he could re-establish contact with me by that method alone."

It is quite obvious that Bholānāth showed an exceptional degree of self-control. It may also be assumed that Nirmalā helped him to live a celibate life by virtue of Her own spiritual power and not just through "shock treatment." Bholānāth himself must have been an unusual person, considering the fact that he was willing to accept this most unconventional marriage. One must bear in mind that his position was particularly anomalous for India, where traditionally women were looked upon as inferior to men. A wife was expected to be submissive to her husband and to worship him as a god. The *Rāmāyaṇa*[7] aptly compares the relation of a wife to her husband to that of a shadow to the substance. Actually Nirmalā's relation to Bholānāth was complex. On the one hand, She was spiritually his superior and later became his *guru* (spiritual teacher). On the other hand, She played the role of an obedient wife. Her mother had enjoined upon Her: "Now you must look upon your husband as your guardian and obey and respect him, just as you did your own parents." Initially She obeyed him in all matters and carried out Her household duties promptly and efficiently. But when Her *kheyāla*[8] inspired Her to act in a certain way, She would brook no opposition. Formally She would always ask his approval before any undertaking, but if his approval was not forthcoming, She would find means to bring about his assent. As Her spiritual status became known and Her lifestyle underwent changes, new problems arose, further challenging the traditional husband-wife relationship. Whenever Ānandamayī Mā decided to travel without Bholānāth, She not only needed his permission to do so but She was required to travel in the company of some respectable elder male, preferably a relative, to preserve "propriety." Also, as people found out about Her exalted spiritual state, they started to come for *darśana* (literally "sight"; being blessed by the presence of a saint). This conflicted with the prevailing rules of *purdāh* (veil or screen; the seclusion of women), according to which a young married woman had to be heavily veiled

[7] One of the great Indian epic narratives.

[8] Normally sudden desire; in Ānandamayī Mā's case, a spontaneous manifestation of divine Will.

and would normally not be in sight of men. Bholānāth proved uncommonly generous in that respect. Under the circumstances he exposed himself to severe criticism from friends and relatives alike. When Nirmalā's spiritual "eccentricities" became more apparent, his relatives urged him to separate from Her and to find a "regular" wife who could provide him with sons, the normal aspiration of every householder. He staunchly resisted these suggestions, even though this was hard for him, given the fact that he was so fond of his family and that there is evidence that he would have liked to have a normal home life. One can only conjecture about his inner conflicts, since he left no memoirs behind. It will, however, become clear from the subsequent events that Ānandamayī Mā subtly molded Her husband-disciple until he was able successfully to cope with all of life's problems. Eventually he must have felt that he was amply compensated for the lack of a conventional family life by reaping a rich spiritual harvest.

How did Ānandamayī Mā regard Her husband? When he once asked Her, in the presence of many of Her devotees, whether She did not love him a little more than others, She retorted emphatically that this was not so. But we do have a statement from Her expressing Her appreciation of Bholānāth: "All of you know that Bholānāth was prone to fits of great anger. It is said that even *ṛṣi*s (saints, seers) were subject to the emotion of anger. Not that I am saying that Bholānāth was a *ṛṣi*. If I did, people would think I was praising my husband. But you have all seen for yourselves that he led an extraordinary life of self-denial and rigorous asceticism."

That Bholānāth was married to a spiritually exalted woman was first recognized during their stay in Astagrāma. Bholānāth and Nirmalā lived in the house of one Sārada Sankar Sen. It was Sen's brother-in-law, Hara Kumār Ray, who "discovered" Her superior spirituality. A well-educated but emotionally unstable person, Hara Kumār Ray was often overtaken by ex-

treme religious fervor and then was unable to attend to his work, some kind of clerical job. Shortly before Nirmalā's arrival in Astagrāma he had lost his mother. It so happened that Nirmalā and Bholānāth occupied the very room where his mother had been living. When he first met Nirmalā he spontaneously prostrated himself in front of Her and addressed Her as "Mā" (mother). From then on he seized every opportunity to be of service to Her. Soon he pleaded with Bholānāth to be permitted to see

Mā daily, to talk to Her, and to receive from Her *prasāda* (food offered to a deity or a saint becomes *prasāda*, when it has been accepted by the deity, and it is subsequently distributed to worshippers). Bholānāth agreed and even told Nirmalā, who had so far not reacted to Hara Kumār Ray's pleading, to talk to him and to give him *prasāda*. One day while paying his worshipful respects to Nirmalā, Hara Kumār exclaimed: "…(now) I am calling you 'Mā,' one day the whole world will call you so," a prophetic statement. Hara Kumār Ray vanished from Mā's life as suddenly as he had appeared. Later on She received a few letters from him in which he addressed Her as *devī* (goddess). Hara Kumār was not the only person in Astagrāma who sensed that Nirmalā was not just an ordinary human being. One of Bholānāth's friends, Ksetra Mohan, also prostrated himself before Her and addressed Her as "Goddess Durgā." Further attention was drawn to the Mother when She entered a trance during a *kīrtana*. So far Her trances had occurred in the privacy of their home. In this instance it was observed by many of the villagers.

In 1916 Mā became seriously ill and was moved to Vidyakut near Kheorā where Her parents were living at that time. During Her stay in Vidyakut Mā showed that She was able to discriminate between genuine spiritual attainment and mere posing. One of Her cousins, Annapūrna, had spells of trance-like states, and the gullible village folk started worshipping her. When Mā encountered Annapūrna in a "trance," She immediately knew that Annapūrna was far from having an ecstatic experience, but that the trance-like state was brought about by her grief over the absence of her husband. She "cured" Her cousin by whispering into her ear that Annapūrna would soon receive a letter from her beloved. In later years the Mother "cured" other seeming saints, and She strongly warned against false *sādhu*s[9] and spiritual fraud in general. Mā remained with Her parents in Vidya-

kut until 1918 when She joined Bholānāth in Bajītpur. He had found employment on one of the estates of the Nawab[10] of Dacca. The next six years (1918-1924), the Bajītpur phase, is usually referred to as the "play of *sādhanā*."[11] Concerning Her *sādhanā*, She explained in retrospect to one of Her devotees: "Let me tell you that what I am, I have been from my infancy. But when the different stages of *sādhanā* were being manifested through this body there was something like superimposition of *ajñāna* (ignorance). But what sort of *ajñāna* was that? It was really *jñāna* (knowledge) masquerading as *ajñāna*…" She further elaborated on the unusual nature of Her *sādhanā*: "One day in Bajītpur I went to bathe in a pond near the house where we lived. While I was pouring water over my body, the *kheyāla* suddenly came to me, 'How would it be to play the role of a *sādhika* (one who practices *sādhanā*).' And so the *līlā* began."

The question why Self-realized masters practice *sādhanā* has been debated in Indian religious literature. In the case of Ramakrishna his devotees maintain that he engaged in *sādhanā* voluntarily as an inspiration to his disciples. From the available account of his life it appears that he had to make a determined effort to gain union with the One. In particular he struggled to free himself from the concept of God in the form of Mother Kālī to reach the formless *Brahman* (Absolute). Moreover he had the guidance of various *guru*s throughout his *sādhanā*. Very different is the case of the Mother. There is no evidence of striving to attain anything. She never had a *guru*. Also, She was totally unacquainted with religious scriptures. We thus witness the spontaneous unfoldment of a *līlā*, rather than a *sādhanā*. At night the Mother would be seen sitting in a corner of their room uttering various *mantra*s and assuming countless complicated *āsana*s (postures). She comments: "When the different stages of

---

[9] One who has dedicated his life to spiritual endeavor.

[10] Deputy; a Muslim administrative title.

[11] Spiritual discipline for the purpose of attaining Self-realization.

sādhanā were being manifested through this body, what a variety of experiences I then had! Sometimes I used to hear distinctly: 'Repeat this *mantra*.' When I got the *mantra* a query arose in me: 'Whose *mantra* is this?' At once the reply came: 'It is the *mantra* of Gaṇesh (elephant-headed god, son of Śiva) or of Viṣṇu,' or something like that. Again the query came from myself: 'How does he look?' A form was revealed in no time. Every question was met by a prompt reply and there was immediate dissolution of all doubts and misgivings. One day I distinctly got the command: 'From today you are not to bow down to anybody.' I asked my invisible monitor: 'Who are you?' The reply came: 'Your *śakti* (power).' I thought that there was a distinct *śakti* residing in me and guiding me by issuing commands from time to time. Since all this happened at the stage of *sādhanā*, *jñāna* was being revealed in a piece-meal fashion. The integral knowledge which this body was possessed of from the very beginning was broken, as it were, into parts and there was something like the superimposition of ignorance.... After some time I again heard the voice within myself which told me: 'Whom do you want to make obedience to? You are everything.' At once I re-

alized that the universe was all my own manifestation. Partial knowledge then gave place to the integral, and I found myself face to face with the One that appears as many. It was then that I understood why I had been forbidden for so long to bow to anybody." During that period various *vibhūti*s (supernormal powers) manifested. She cured people from all sorts of diseases by merely touching them.

The nightly spectacle of Mā's *sādhanā* filled Bholānāth with extreme awe. The ecstatically blissful Mā chanted often for hours, repeating the name of Hari (name for Viṣṇu). This displeased Bholānāth who was not a *vaiṣṇava* like his wife, but a *śākta* (worshipper of Śiva's consort, Kālī or Durgā). He therefore urged Mā to chant the name of Śiva or Kālī. She instantly complied with his request, fully cognizant of the fact that all divine names are equally effective.

In the beginning Mā engaged in *sādhanā* only at night when no one but Bholānāth could observe Her. Soon, however, *mantra*s and Sanskrit stanzas flowed from Her lips in the presence of outsiders. Witnessing Her unconventional behavior, the neighbors became suspicious and some even concluded that the Mother of Smiles was possessed by evil spirits. No longer did She enjoy unqualified popularity. Bholānāth was placed in an awkward position, experiencing the pressure of friends and neighbors to put an end to the improper behavior of his wife. He felt compelled to summon several *ojhā*s (spirit exorcisers) to "cure" his wife. One *ojhā* received a drastic lesson while trying to free Mā from evil spirits. When he touched Her he was seized with such a pain that he fell writhing to the ground. Upon Bholānāth's pleading, Mā removed the pain, whereupon the *ojhā* prostrated himself in front of Her and then left in a hurry. Eventually Bholānāth consulted a distinguished physician, Dr. Mahendra C. Nandi. After observing Mā, he assured Bholānāth that She did not suffer from mental illness but showed obvious signs of being God-intoxicated. This reminds one of Ramakrishna who too was

Ānandamayī Mā in *samādhi*

for a time suspected of mental imbalance while actually experiencing divine ecstasy. Even in spiritual India, worldliness is the normal state of mankind, and extreme God-centeredness is so rare that it is understandably considered madness. A comparison of Mā's *sādhanā* with that of Ramakrishna shows that both went rapidly through spiritual disciplines which normally require a lifetime of practice, and both followed various Hindu as well as non-Hindu religious practices. In the case of Mā, however, except for a few vague statements, no details regarding the performance of non-Hindu rites are available. It was the night of *jhūlan pūrṇimā*.[12] She had prepared Her husband's evening meal and had just started Her customary nocturnal worship, when She received the inspiration to enact the role of a *guru* and of a *śiṣya* (disciple) simultaneously. The *bīja mantra* (seed *mantra*; *mantra* of initiation) proceeded from Her lips spontaneously and She repeated it with the realization that *guru*, *śiṣya*, and *mantra* were one. Mā explained the underlying meaning of initiation: "God Himself in the role of the spiritual preceptor (*guru*) discloses His name to the pilgrim wandering in search of a guide." There is no other known instance of self-initiation. This lends further weight to the view that in the person of Mā we are faced with a unique phenomenon.

During the months following Mā's initiation, Her *sādhanā* grew in intensity. She tells us that She had visions of various deities of the Hindu pantheon. Bholānāth often observed that She identified Herself with a particular deity and subsequently worshipped that very deity. Underlying all Her worship was the theme of Oneness: worshipper, worshipping, and the object of Her worship merged. During that phase She was hardly conscious of Her body and only occasionally touched food or felt the need to sleep.

[12] August full moon festival in which images of the divine lovers Kṛṣṇa and Rādhā are placed in swings.

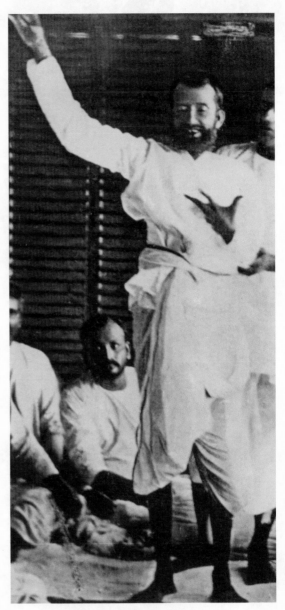

Ramakrishna in *samādhi*

Naturally there was concern and even indignation among some of Her relatives when Her unconventional behavior continued. One of Her cousins in particular was shocked that She had initiated Herself while Her husband had not yet been initiated. The head of the household was thus placed in a position spiritually inferior to his wife. When the cousin challenged Mā, She assured him that Bholānāth

would receive initiation in five months' time. Early in December 1922, She Herself initiated Her husband—another break with spiritual convention. In this connection it should be stressed that She carried out the initiation ceremony in accordance with the rules laid down in the *Śāstra*s (Scriptures), even though She was not acquainted with them.

Following Bholānāth's initiation, for a period of three years, Mā remained in complete silence, which She only rarely interrupted for the purpose of either comforting someone in deep distress or to convey an important message. While She was still in silence, Bholānāth lost his position in Bajītpur and decided to move to Dacca, the chief city in East Bengal, in April, 1924. In Dacca the chances of finding permanent employment seemed more favorable than in the villages or small towns where they had lived up to that time. On April 17th, 1924, Bholānāth secured work with his former employer, the Nawab of Dacca. He was appointed manager of the Nawab's extensive estate, the Shah-bagh gardens. There in a small house Mā's *līlā* continued. It so happened that several acquaintances from Bajītpur had also moved to Dacca. Through them the news about Mā's exalted status spread rapidly, attracting the first real devotees to the "Mother of Shah-bagh gardens." Among them were Prān Gopāl Mukherji, Deputy Postmaster General of Dacca and family, Nishikanta Mitra, a *zamindār* (landowner) and family, Nani Gopāl Banerji, a professor at Dacca College, Baul Chandra Basak, lecturer at Vakil Institute. It is significant that all of the devotees were *bhadralok*s (respectable people, gentlemen, a privileged minority from the highest castes, usually landed or professionals, always well educated) who came to sit at the feet of the practically illiterate Mā. One is reminded of another *bhadralok*, Pratap Candra Māzumdar, who explained why he, a westernized intellectual, sat at the feet of the illiterate Ramakrishna: "His religion is ecstasy, his worship means transcendental insight...." Similarly, being in the presence of the "Mother of Shah-bagh gardens" seemed transcendental bliss to Her followers.

We are fortunate to have an account by a Dr. Nalini Kanta Brahma of his visit to Shah-bagh, which enables us to recapture at least to some extent the atmosphere prevailing there. "It was a cold evening in December 1924, when I was taken to Shah-bagh for a *darśana* of the Mother by Rai Bahadur Prān Gopāl Mukherji, the then Deputy Postmaster General of Dacca. He had already secured the permission of Her husband for the purpose and we were taken straight to the room where Mother was sitting alone deeply absorbed in meditation. A dim lamp was burning in front of Her and that was perhaps the only thing in the room. Mother's face was completely hidden from our view as in those days She used to veil it exactly like a newly married village girl.... After we had waited there for about half an hour, suddenly the veil loosened itself and Mother's face became visible in all its brilliance and luster. Hymns containing many seed *mantra*s began to be recited by the Mother in uncommon accents, producing wonderful resonance, which affected the whole surroundings. The stillness of the cold December night, the loneliness of the Shah-bagh gardens, and above all the sublimity and serenity of the atmosphere in the Mother's room—all combined to produce a sense of holiness. As long as we were in the room, we felt an indescribable elevation of the spirit, a silence and a depth not previously experienced, a peace that passeth all understanding ..."

While in Shah-bagh, Mā was seen to be more frequently than ever in trancelike states. On several occasions Her husband found Her unconscious, on the point of drowning in the pond near their house into which She had fallen while cleaning the kitchenware. Bholānāth concluded that he could not leave Her all by Herself at home. He asked his widowed sister, Mātarī, whom Mā had befriended while living in his eldest brother's home, to stay with them and look after his wife. Mā became increasingly friendly with Mātarī. Their close relationship lasted until Mātarī's death in 1959. Meanwhile, in August 1924, Mā's younger sister Surabalā had died at the age of sixteen. Assuming that Mā must be deeply grieved by the death of Her sister, Bholānāth arranged for Her parents to join the household in Shah-bagh. It was his

hope that the presence of Her parents would help Mā bear the loss of Her sister. Little did he as yet understand Nirmalā, for whom death held no dread. Conscious of the oneness of all existence, Mā was totally unaffected by the *līlā* of life and death: "Come what may, what does it matter?"

Mā's first year in Shah-bagh is also memorable for the discovery of Siddheśvarī. During Her stay in Bajītpur She had had a vision of a sacred site in the neighborhood of Dacca by the name of Siddheśvarī. Upon inquiry in Dacca She was finally led to an abandoned, almost inaccessible Kālī temple in the midst of a wilderness. Further investigation revealed that Siddheśvarī had numerous associations with great saints and sages of the past. Śaṅkarācārya (788-820 A.D.), the greatest exponent of *advaita* (monism) is supposed to have spent some time there. From September 1924 on, Mā frequently stayed overnight in the Kālī temple of Siddheśvarī. In 1928 an *āśram* was built at Siddheśvarī, the first of a network of *āśram*s all over northern India, to be nuclei for worship and the spreading of Mā's teaching.

Meanwhile the little house in Shah-bagh became a veritable magnet for *darśana* seekers. Bholānāth intuitively knew that he must disregard conventions and set aside all feelings of possessiveness to make Mā accessible to the public. When Her silence ended in October 1925, he let the devotees talk freely with Her. Bholānāth ignored Mā's warning: "You must think twice before you open the doors to the world in this manner. Remember that you will not be able to stem the tide when it becomes overwhelming." And the tide was approaching, threatening to engulf what little privacy the young couple had enjoyed.

Mā's first public appearance occurred in connection with Kālī *pūjā*, the festival in honor of the Divine Mother in Her terrifying aspect which is confined to Bengal. Reluctantly She had agreed to conduct the Kālī *pūjā* in 1925. During the ceremony She deviated from com-

mon practice by placing flowers and sandal paste upon Her own head instead of the idol, obviously implying that She was the true reflection of Kālī and not the image. It is reported that: "All that time Mother's face glowed with an intense uncommon beauty and throughout the ceremony there was a spell of great sanctity and deep absorption over all the people present." She did permit the sacrifice of a goat as was customary on this occasion, but She saw to it that in subsequent Kālī *pūjā* celebrations in which She participated no animal was sacrificed. The true meaning of animal sacrifice, She explained, was sacrificing one's lower (animal) nature, living up to the fact that it was man's destiny to raise himself to his inherent divine status.

Mā's *līlā* assumed constantly new features, mystifying, thrilling, often overwhelming Her devotees. On January 26, 1926, a *kīrtana* was performed at Shah-bagh on the occasion of the solar eclipse. We have a most vivid description of the happenings at the *kīrtana*: "At one moment Mātājī was sitting like one of us. The next moment She had changed completely. Her body started swaying rhythmically.... With Her body still swaying, She stood up or rather was drawn upwards on Her toes. It looked as if Mātājī had left Her body which had become an instrument in the hands of an invisible power.... She circled round the room as if wafted along by the wind. Occasionally, Her body would start falling to the ground—but before it completed the movement it would regain its upright position, just like a wind-blown leaf which flutters towards the ground and then is uplifted and blown forward by a fresh gust of wind. It seemed Her body had no weight or substance.... Before the crowd had time to realize that She was in their midst, She fell to the ground from an upright position but did not appear to be hurt at all. Like a leaf in a whirlwind, Her body started rolling at tremendous speed while She was lying prostrate.... After a few moments, Her body of its own accord stopped moving and Mātājī sat up. Now She was still like a statue.... Her face was flushed and radiant and there was an effulgence all around Her." After a while She sang with a heavenly voice:

> O Hari, O Murāri, O foe of Kaiṭabha and Mādhu.
> O Gopāl, O Govinda, O Mukunda, O Śauri![13]

At Mā's suggestion nightly *kīrtana*s were instituted at Shah-bagh. At those *kīrtana*s She exhibited varying aspects of rapture. Watching the nocturnal miraculous events, the devotees became convinced that Her body was possessed by divine forces for the purpose of manifesting the infinite beauty of the cosmic creation. Not only *kīrtana*s but specific events in nature, such

as the sight of rippling waves, brought about ecstatic states in the Mother. Here again one can find a similarity in the life of Ramakrishna who experienced ecstasy at the sight of a thundercloud.

In October, 1926, Mā was again asked to perform Kālī *pūjā*. Once more She deviated from the normal ritual. When the *pūjā* was drawing to a close and *pūrṇāhuti* (the final burnt offering of a sacrifice) arrived, She did not permit it to be offered. Instead She suggested that the sacrificial fire be preserved—it is still kept burning at Her *āśram*s in Dehradun and Naimishāraṇya, and in Vārāṇasi where it

---

[13] Kaiṭabha and Mādhu were two demons killed by Viṣṇu. All other names are various epithets of Viṣṇu or Kṛṣṇa.

was transferred at the time of the Partition in 1947.[14] As a rule, at the conclusion of a *pūjā*, the image is immersed in the holy Ganges. At the request of a devotee, the Mother, however, gave instructions to keep the idol. It was later placed in Her *āśram* at Ramna (near the race course in Dacca) and on Her birthday it was made accessible for *darśana* to people of all castes and creeds. Mā thus made a liberalizing innovation approximately ten years ahead of Mahatma Gandhi's campaign for opening temples to all castes.

The regular performance of Hindu rites on the Nawab's property did not encounter opposition from the Muslims. In fact Mā gained the respect and affection of the Nawab's family and of Muslims in general. The Muslim community had good reasons to be fond of the Mother of Shah-bagh gardens, as She frequently gave indications of Her reverence for Islam. In Shah-bagh there happened to be the grave of a Muslim *faqīr*. Once Ānandamayī Mā was seen performing *namāz* (Muslim prayer) at his grave. Spontaneously a prayer issued from Her lips which was identified by some bystanders as Arabic verses from the Koran. During a *kīrtana*, Ānandamayī Mā noticed a Muslim watching Her from a distance. She moved towards him with a welcoming gesture, chanting: "*Allah, Allahu Akbar* (God is great)." On another occasion She walked up to some Muslim workmen and got them to chant in unison the praises of Allah. Gradually She acquired a number of devoted Muslim disciples. Even after the Partition, when Mā could no longer visit Her homeland, East Bengal, She retained a core of loyal Muslim followers there. They looked after Her *āśram*s and provided the necessary financial means for their upkeep. As far as Mā is concerned, Hindus and Muslims or adherents of other religions ultimately are one: "*Kīrtana* and *namāz* are one and the same."[15]

Ānandamayī Mā at a shrine

While Mā was attracting Muslims, the majority of Her followers were Hindus. In 1925-26 some of Her greatest devotees, who constituted the inner circle of Her ever expanding spiritual family, were drawn to Her. In the beginning of 1926, Dr. Sasanka Mohan Mukhopadhyaya, a retired Civil Surgeon and his second eldest daughter Adarini Devī (now known as Gurupriyā Devī or Didi, i.e. elder sister) came to Her. Dr. Mukhopadhyaya, who had been used to worldly comforts, eventually became a renunciant under the Mother's purifying influence. Didi, a deeply religious girl, had thwarted her parents' earlier plans to have her

[14] The same fire was used for the great sacrifice from 1947-1950.

[15] Editor's Note: According to a Muslim devotee, "Although Mā was born into a Hindu family, She is also the Mā of the Muslims. She is our own Mā." (from Bithika Mukerji in "Śrī Ānandamayī Mā: Divine Play of the Spiritual Journey," in *Hindu Spirituality: Vedas through Vedanta*, in *World Spirituality*, Krishna Swaraman, ed., vol. 6 [New York: Crossroad, 1989], p. 395, quoted by Lisa Lassell Hallstrom in *Mother of Bliss: Ānandamayī Mā (1896-1982)* [New York: Oxford University Press, 1999], p. 26)

married. She immediately attracted Mā's attention: "Where have you been all this time?" This reminds one of Ramakrishna's similar exclamation upon meeting Narendranath Datta, the future Swami Vivekananda. Didi became Mā's close assistant and helped Her first with household duties and later with the administration of the various *āśram*s. It is to her that we owe the most extensive record of Ānandamayī Mā's

Ānandamayī Mā with Didi (Gurupriyā Devī)

līlā—a total of seventeen volumes in Bengali and nineteen in Hindi chronicling the daily events in Her life have been published so far. If Didi can be considered Her most intimate woman devotee, Her most advanced man devotee was Jyotiścandra Ray, later known as Bhāijī (brother), Personal Assistant to the Director of Agriculture of Bengal. Bhāijī met Her towards the end of 1924. Shortly afterwards Ānandamayī Mā told him: "There is a very subtle close spiritual link between this body and yourself." Towards the end of his life Bhāijī wrote what is probably the most insightful account of his experiences with Mā, entitled *Mother as Revealed to Me*. In it he relates the genesis of the name Ānandamayī Mā. One afternoon, while he was busy at work, the Mother summoned him to Shah-bagh. Upon his arrival there She informed him that he was to accompany Her and Bholānāth to Siddheśvarī. While She was sitting near the Kālī temple at Siddheśvarī it occurred to him all of a sudden to suggest to Bholānāth: "From today we shall call Mother by the name of Ānandamayī." Bholānāth instantly agreed. The following day, when he asked the Mother why She had ordered him to interrupt his office duties, She responded laughingly: "If you had not come, who else would have given a name to this body." A remark such as this leads one to conclude that the bliss-permeated Mother is perfectly attuned to the cosmic *līlā*—everything unfolds at the proper time and under the proper circumstances. Hamlet-like doubt is alien to Her. She often says: "Whatever is to be, will be."

Around this time (1926), people started coming regularly to Ānandamayī Mā, expecting Her to cure them from physical ailments. She made it clear to Her devotees that She could not indiscriminately effect cures, but only when She was "prompted" to do so. There were times when She had distinct indications that She was not to heal. In such cases She simply informed the person in question that it was not his destiny to be cured by Her. Discussing the

Ānandamayī Mā with Bholānāth (right) and Bhāijī (left)

subject of healing and other so-called super-natural powers, She explained that such powers often come to spiritual seekers as a byproduct of their *sādhanā*. But powers *per se* must never become the goal. One should accept such manifestations humbly and with equanimity, always keeping in mind that God-realization is the only worthwhile objective.

Ānandamayī Mā continued to be a constant reminder of the fact that unlimited powers can be manifested through the instrumentality of the human body. Already in Bajītpur, She

had surprised Her devotees by eating unusually small amounts of food. Some time in 1924, She lost Her ability to feed Herself. Her fingers simply refused to hold on to food. No "satisfactory" explanation is available to account for the loss of what normally is considered a vital function. Yet it appears that Her "handicap" may perhaps be meant to demonstrate that eating is less of a basic need than man ordinarily thinks. From that time on, the bliss-permeated Mother has been fed by others, first by Bholānāth and then chiefly by Didi. Recently, other younger devotees have taken over this duty. Feeding Ānandamayī Mā has been problematic. Initially She accepted absurdly small quantities of food or refused to eat altogether. Once She abstained from all food and drink for twenty-three days. This is most unusual, considering that the great Gandhi took in at least some liquid while fasting. For half a year Ānandamayī Mā lived on a daily diet of six grains of boiled rice and two or three ripe fruits which—She insisted—must have fallen from trees. If no fruit had fallen off in a natural way, She would forgo eating fruit on that day. The disconcerting thing about Ānandamayī Mā was that well-meaning devotees found out that it was impossible to deceive Her and pretend that a fruit had fallen off a tree. Once, after She had not touched any food for days, Bholānāth expressed his concern for Her well-being. The next day She ate all the *purees* (fried unleavened brown bread) that were available, completely exhausting the household supply of flour and *ghee* (clarified butter). And She warned: "Had there been more I would have eaten them all. I tell you, do not make arrangements for me. If I really start eating none of you will be able to provide for me, however rich you may be." In fact, once She ate forty pounds of pudding meant for a large party. Yet She suffered none of the consequences attendant upon gluttony. The bliss-permeated Mother is a concrete example of what Heinrich Zimmer calls "the phenomenon of expanding form."[16] Just as in Hindu mythology the pigmy Vāman manages with one step to reach beyond the sun, so too Ānandamayī Mā can, if She desires, eat superhuman quantities of food. Essentially She tries to teach by example that humanity is far too food-conscious, and that most people grossly overeat. The body requires only a small amount of food. The remainder, eaten out of habit, because it is pleasurable, is wasted. Through *yoga*,[17] She avers, man can free himself from dependence upon food and imbibe by spiritual means the necessary energy from his surroundings. Being conscious of the Oneness underlying the multiple manifestation, She is able to extract whatever She "needs" out of "air." Thus She is a living example of Christ's saying that "Man does not live by bread alone." Hoarding of food draws Her special censure. Noticing an undue amount of stocked food in the home of a Calcutta devotee, She went to his storage room and had all the food distributed among the neighborhood families.

[16] Heinrich Zimmer, *Myths and Symbols in Indian Art and Civilization* (Harper Torchbooks, 1962).

[17] Literally "union." Various methods of realizing the union of the individual self with the universal Self.

Ānandamayī Mā could not only transcend the need for food whenever She so desired, but, according to Bhāijī, She could often be seen in the breathless state of *samādhi*.[18] He describes one of those instances: "Her face glowed with a crimson hue due to the intensity of inner *ānandam* (bliss): Her cheeks shone with a heavenly light, Her forehead looked bright and serene with a divine calm. All Her physical expressions were suspended; yet from every pore of Her body radiated an uncommon glow—a mute eloquence of silent, inner speech. Everybody present felt that Mother was sinking into the depths of divine communion. Thus passed some ten to twelve hours...." Bhāijī was also fortunate to be present when Ānandamayī Mā revealed that She had had a direct experience of man's spiritual anatomy. She had clearly seen the working of the *cakra*s (the subtle spiritual centers) along the spine and in the brain. Not only did She draw figures of the *cakra*s but She explained in detail their functioning during man's spiritual advance. Years later Bhāijī compared Ānandamayī Mā's drawings of the *cakra*s with those found in Sir John George Woodroffe's *Serpent Power* and found that they were in agreement. When he wanted to show the book to Ānandamayī Mā, She did not even look at it. Instead the illiterate Ānandamayī Mā revealed to him details about the *cakra*s not known to the western scholar.

Gradually, the unusual phenomena in Ānandamayī Mā's life receded into the background. The "*sādhanā*" phase was over by the end of 1926. Even before that Ānandamayī Mā had extended the field of Her activity beyond the Dacca area. She embarked upon travels throughout East Bengal and even all over Northern India. In May, 1926, for instance, She visited the temple sites of Deogarh in Bihar at the request of Her devotee Prān Gopal Mukherji, the former Deputy Postmaster General of Dacca, who had retired to Deogarh to live there close to the *āśram* of his *guru*, Balānanda Brahmachari Māharaj. Mukherji introduced Mā to Balānanda. The renowned sage was deeply impressed by Her and exclaimed that he regarded Her as the Divine Mother incarnate. Through Balānanda other *māhātmā*s (great souls) flocked to Her. Wherever She went from now on She attracted magnet-like the saints and sages of India. Soon after Her return from Deogarh, She ceased to cover Her face with the folds of Her sari. Her whole being now exuded confidence, so that people felt the urge to bring their spiritual problems to Her. The counseling phase of Her life was under way.

---

[18] State in which the mind is fused with the object of contemplation (e.g. the Lord) and becomes luminious, taking on its form.

Above: The Ganges at Hardwar; *Below*: the ghats at Vārāṇasi

Above: The Ganges at Hrishikesh; *Below*: the Bengali ghat at Māthura

Early in 1927 Ānandamayī Mā and Her entourage visited the sacred pilgrimage centers of Hrishikesh and Hardwar in the Himalayas. While in Hardwar She ordered Didi and her father to stay there for three months and practice *sādhanā* in solitude. She had decided that the time had come to eradicate whatever worldly traits were still lingering in those two close devotees. In the austere simplicity of the Himalayas they were to live a life of renunciation. Considering that Sasanka Mohan Mukherjee was an elderly man and that he was used to comforts (for Indian circumstances), he showed remarkable hardiness. He had to get accustomed to walking long distances over rugged terrain and to bathing in cold streams. The spiritual path is not meant for weaklings. The bliss-permeated Mother, meanwhile, continued Her travels, stopping at Māthura and Vrindaban, the sites of Lord Kṛṣṇa's earthly *līlā*, and Vārāṇasi the spiritual capital of India, before returning to Dacca.

The devotees in Dacca were gradually becoming aware of the fact that their monopoly on Mā was a matter of the past. Ever more frequently did She go on extended trips. In July, 1927, Her *kheyāla* prompted Her to go to Vindhyācal in Uttar Pradesh. At that time

Ānandamayī Mā at the Vindhyācal *āśram*

Vindhyācal consisted of a few huts in the midst of a jungle. When they reached Vindhyācal, Ānandamayī Mā walked around as though in a trance. She explained that it was hallowed

Temple at Vindhyācal

ground, permeated by the vibrations of numerous saints of former ages. The government was notified that it ought to undertake excavations in the region of Vindhyācal. Eventually several temple ruins were uncovered precisely where Mā had sensed an especially holy atmosphere. Vindhyācal became one of Her favorite sites for retreats. An *āśram* was erected there, serving as another link in the chain of centers animated by Ānandamayī Mā's spirituality.

In April, 1927, on the occasion of Ānandamayī Mā's thirty-first birthday, Bhāijī suggested that special *kīrtana* and *pūjā* be performed in Her honor. Henceforth elaborate birthday celebrations have been regularly held, lasting over a week and attended by large crowds. Some may wonder why the egoless Ānandamayī Mā, who is beyond time and space, permits the celebration of Her birthdays. After all, according to the *Bhagavad Gītā*:[19] "Nor I, nor thou, nor any one of these, ever was not, nor ever will not be." On Her sixtieth birthday commemoration, in 1956, when a devotee asked Her about the meaning of Her birthday, She replied that it was true that She was not born, nor was Lord Kṛṣṇa for that matter, and yet His birthday is being celebrated. Such birthdays, consisting entirely of religious functions, serve to focus people's attention on the Divine and thereby increase their devotion and spiritual receptivity.

Bhāijī was not only responsible for initiating special birthday functions for Mā but he

19 The Lord's Song. An episode from the Hindu epic *Mahābhārata*, in which Lord Kṛṣṇa reveals the nature of reality to Arjuna.

Ānandamayī Mā lying in *samadhi* at top of shrine during her 59th birthday ceremony; Almora *āśram*

also made chants to "Mā" an integral part of *kīrtana*s in Her *āśram*s: "Merge all names and forms in the 'Mā' *mantra*, Say always Mā, Mā, and let your eyes swim in floods of tears, Find in Śrī Ānandamayī Mā the final refuge of your life's journey," was one of the chants composed by Bhāijī.

Three months after the celebration of Her thirty-first birthday, on August 3rd, 1927, the bliss-permeated Mother visited Her birthplace, Kheorā, accompanied by Bholānāth and Her mother, normally referred to as Didimā (grandmother). Their erstwhile home had been sold to Muslims who had changed it almost beyond recognition, so that Didimā found it difficult to orient herself in it. Ānandamayī Mā, however, went straight to an enclosure where cow dung was kept and identified it as the spot where She had been born. Then something totally unexpected happened. She picked up a piece of earth from that very site while tears were flooding Her eyes. How is one to interpret this show of emotion coming from the even-minded Ānandamayī Mā who, as a rule, is detached from life and death, joy and sorrow? Maybe this behavior will appear less puzzling if we keep in mind that, according to Hindu philosophy, God is both in and beyond manifestation; thus while He is beyond duality, He also manifests as duality. It is also known that the great *avatāras*[20] voluntarily take on human limitations. Perhaps, at this juncture of Her *līlā*, Ānandamayī Mā saw fit to play the role of a common mortal with emotional attachment to Her place of birth which She had not seen for seventeen years. One must also bear in mind that Ānandamayī Mā already knew that She would soon leave Her homeland, Bengal, where She would return for brief visits only. She may have wanted to give Her devotees advance notice of the impending change and chose a symbolic gesture for this purpose.

[20] Descent of the Divine, usually in one of its aspects or powers.

Early in 1928 Bholānāth lost his job in Shah-bagh. For the time being, whenever they were not traveling, Ānandamayī Mā, Bholānāth, Her parents, and Aunt Mātari rented a house in the Tikatuli district of Dacca. In September, 1928, during a visit to Vārāṇasi, She met Māhāmahopādhyāya Gopināth Kavirāj, one of India's greatest Sanskrit scholars, then Principal of Queen's College in Vārāṇasi. He became one of Her foremost devotees and is responsible for many publications about Ānandamayī Mā. At Vārāṇasi Mā was practically inundated by crowds of *darśana* seekers. Whatever had remained of Her "private" life was swallowed up by Her duties to those who sought spiritual solace from Her. Bholānāth had to adjust himself to a life that included few of the normal aspects of a householder's existence. In December, 1928, Ānandamayī Mā decided that the time had come to intensify Bholānāth's *sādhanā*. She told him to go for solitary meditation to Tārāpeeth, a sacred site whose cremation grounds are ideally suited for yogic practices.

The temporary absence of Bholānāth raised the question who was to "look after" Ānandamayī Mā. One still felt the need to uphold certain properties. How could a woman be without a guardian? It was decided to designate Didi's father as Her "guardian." Although She was recognized to be a great saint, if not the Divine Mother in the flesh, She still was subject to certain restrictions as a woman. Obviously holiness did not entirely make up for a woman's inferior status. Many men admitted that they initially had to face the taunts of their relatives for sitting at the feet of a mere woman.

Whatever their relatives might say, devotees of Ānandamayī Mā could not resist the magnetism of Her personality. When Her birthday was celebrated in May, 1929, the Siddheśvarī *āśram* was found inadequate to accommodate all Her followers. The celebrations were therefore held at the newly completed *āśram* in Ramna. At the end of the birthday ceremonies Ānandamayī Mā abruptly announced that She

The Ramna *āśram* at Dacca

by that time. In addition, his relatives urged him at long last to assert his position as head of the household. He mustered all his courage and remonstrated with Ānandamayī Mā. What ensued is best described in Her own words: "I tried to cook for a few days with mother's help.... I had no objections and it made no difference to me ... (but) Bholānāth fell ill after a few days, and then I myself was ill. So it did not after all come to anything at all." Evidently the household *līlā* was over, while Bholānāth's education continued.

Not only was Bholānāth deprived of Her cooking skills, he had to give up one more physical comfort which he had so far still enjoyed: sleeping in a bed. Some time in October, 1929, when Ānandamayī Mā was again in poor health, She made him leave his bed in the middle of the night, ostensibly because She wanted to occupy it. He had to lie on the floor in a blanket, the way She was wont to sleep. This more austere mode of sleeping became a permanent arrangement for Bholānāth, for within a few days Ānandamayī Mā had his bed taken apart while She returned to sleeping on the floor.

At the time when Ānandamayī Mā was further disciplining Bholānāth, She experienced Her first encounter with the academic commu-

would leave Dacca that very night. Bholānāth was to stay at Ramna *āśram*. In conformity with Her role as an obedient wife, She asked Bholānāth's permission to leave, although She made it unmistakably clear that permission had to be granted: "If you say, 'no,' I shall leave this body at your feet just now." She was amenable, however, to Bholānāth's request that She travel in the company of Her father. Otherwise: "People will speak ill of you...," he had pleaded.

Ānandamayī Mā left Ramna around midnight by the next available train which took Her to Mymensingh in East Bengal. From there She traveled to Cox Bazar (East Bengal) and then to Hardwar, Dehradun (in the Himalayas), Ayodhya (Uttar Pradesh), and Vārāṇasi. She did not inform Bholānāth about Her moves. Shortly after Her return to Dacca, She was no longer able to hold on to kitchen utensils and consequently had to relinquish all household work. This new development was more than Bholānāth was willing to bear. After all, he was still very human. Feelings of frustration had accumulated

Temple in Dhakeshwari, Dacca

nity. When a congress of Indian philosophers was convened in Dacca in 1929, some of the delegates visited Ānandamayī Mā. For hours the uneducated Mā answered spontaneously the most profound questions thrown at Her by the erudite scholars. Her "reputation" was

firmly established and members of the learned professions came to Her in increasing numbers. There followed a period of travels seemingly at random all over Northern India. Then, in August, 1930, Mā ventured on Her first visit to Southern India, all the way to Cape Comorin. Although She did not speak any of the South Indian languages, She was received with reverence wherever She traveled. She showed great fascination for the vastly different culture of the South and gave occasional hints that She was quite "at home" in South India, that She was on familiar ground.

One more birthday was celebrated in Dacca in May/June 1932. Previously, whenever She had left Dacca, She had assured Her devotees that She would return to that city. But on the night of June 2, 1932, She informed Didi about Her intention to leave Dacca permanently. Any attempt to dissuade Her from Her plan would be in vain: "Let me move about according to my *kheyāla*. I cannot do so if you all put obstacles in my path." At 11.30 p.m. She had Bhāijī summoned. Except for Bholānāth he was the only one to accompany Her. Bhāijī had to make a momentous decision. He realized that following Ānandamayī Mā meant severing his family ties. He pleaded for time to fetch money from his home but was told that they would leave immediately. With hardly any baggage the three departed from Dacca. True renunciation is clearly not compatible with concern for worldly ballast. At the railroad station Ānandamayī Mā asked for tickets "right up to the terminus of the line," which happened to be Jagannathgunj. From there they proceeded to the Himalayas. Uninterrupted traveling followed. Only towards the end of 1935 did Ānandamayī Mā revisit Dacca for four days. Like "a bird on the wing" She has been traveling ever since, staying only for a few days, at most a few weeks, at any one place. "I find one vast garden spread out all over the universe. All plants, all human beings, all higher mind-bodies are about in this garden in various ways, each has its own unique-

ness and beauty. Their presence and variety give me great delight. Every one of you adds with his special feature to the glory of the garden. I move about from one place to another in the same garden. What makes you feel my absence so keenly when I happen to leave your part of the garden for another, to gladden your brothers over there?" Wherever She goes *kīrtana*s and *pūjā*s are celebrated. The focus is always on the Divine.

While originally Ānandamayī Mā spoke only Bengali, She gradually acquired facility in Hindi. Although there remains an inner core of Bengali devotees, many non-Bengali Indians and even foreigners can now be counted among Her devotees. Followers include businessmen, artists, scholars, journalists, *mahātmā*s (great souls), *rājā*s (kings) and *rānī*s (queens), as well as government leaders. Already in 1933 Kamala Nehru, the wife of Jawarharlal Nehru,[21] visited Her in Dehradun. From that time on Kamala frequently saw Ānandamayī Mā and meditated in Her presence. The bliss-permeated Mother was extremely gracious to Her. Many years later, reminiscing about Kamala, Ānandamayī Mā revealed that Kamala had had exceptionally deep meditations and had been repeatedly blessed with visions of Kṛṣṇa. It was through Kamala Nehru's inspiration that She had requested all Her devotees to set aside at least fifteen minutes daily for divine communion. When Kamala became seriously ill, the bliss-permeated Mother visited her several times in the hospital near Almora. After Kamala's death, a rosary (*japa mālā*) given to her by Ānandamayī Mā was handed on to her daughter, Indira Gandhi, who treasures it to this day.[22] Indira Gandhi as well as her father Jawarharlal Nehru continued to seek Ānandamayī Mā's *darśana*. Kamala was also instrumental in bringing together Mahatma Gandhi and Ānandamayī Mā.

[21] First Prime Minister of India, from 1947 to his death in 1964.

[22] Prime Minister of India from 1966 to 1977, and again from 1980 to her assassination in 1984.

Left: Brahmacārinī Ātmānanda (1904-1985);
Right: Brahmacāri Vijayānanda (b. 1915)

Several meetings ensued. Once Mā participated in one of Gandhiji's prayer meetings. Other well-known Indian devotees include the former President of India, Rajendra Prasad, and the former Vice-President Gopal Svarup Pathak, the former Chief Justice of Mysore, Subdharanjan Dasgupta, Vijayaraje, Maharani of Gwalior, the wealthy industrialist and philanthropist, Jugal Kishore Birla, the singer Dilip Kumar Roy, the dancer Uday Shankar, Professors Tripurari Chakravarti of Calcutta University, Bireshwar Ganguly of Patna University, and Raihana Tyabji, a Muslim woman saint, who was close to Gandhiji.

Among the foreigners who were attracted to Ānandamayī Mā is an Austrian who eventually became a renunciant and is now known under the name of Brahmacārinī Ātmānanda. When she met Ānandamayī Mā, she only knew some colloquial Hindi. Gradually she acquired a perfect knowledge of Bengali and has been instrumental in translating Ānandamayī Mā's teaching into English. Dr. Adolphe Jacques Weintrob, a successful medical practitioner from Marseille, has become Brahmacāri Vijayānanda and lived upon Ānandamayī Mā's instruction in seclusion in Almora for several years and is now at Kankhal. The well-known British photographer Richard Lannoy, the French film producer, Arnaud Desjardins, and the German novelist, Melita Maschmann, also found that

Ānandamayī Mā was the answer to their spiritual longings. Melita Maschmann published a book about her impressions of Ānandamayī Mā under the title, *Der Tiger singt Kirtana*. It is a spiritual masterpiece, showing the great sensitivity of the German writer. An Italian woman, Miriam Orr, became a devotee of Ānandamayī Mā immediately upon seeing a photograph of the bliss-permeated Mother. In recent years Mā has been visited by the Swiss and Chilean ambassadors, the Queen Mother of Greece, and the Canadian Prime Minister, Trudeau.

From 1932 to the present[23] Ānandamayī Mā's *līlā* has been an uninterrupted outpouring of divine counsel, an incessant call to mankind to awaken from the sleep of delusion to the realization of the One who alone is real. The conventional historian will be utterly frustrated by Her unconcern for worldly events. But, after all, is not history the epitome of *māyā*?[24] Thus Gandhiji's non-violent campaign, the independence struggle, the Partition of India are almost totally ignored by Her. She only briefly commented upon the Punjab massacres in 1947, simply stating that they happened because they were bound to happen. When Gandhiji was assassinated She likened his death to Christ's crucifixion. Apart from these two instances, there are no references to political events. Melita Maschmann provides us with a clue to Ānandamayī Mā's apparent disregard of political events. The German novelist stayed with the bliss-permeated Mother during the Cuban missile crisis of 1961. She relates that she was able to retain her calmness throughout the crisis, even though she was aware of the danger inherent in the situation. Being in the presence of Mā helped her to raise her consciousness above the realm of duality, and made her realize that her true Self cannot be touched by anything material. Where bliss reigns, fear must vanish.

[23] Editor's Note: The time of this writing is 1973.

[24] The illusive power by which the One conceals Itself and appears as the many.

Above: Ānandamayī Mā with Indira Gandhi and Pandit Nehru;
Below: Ānandamayī Mā with Former Prime Minister of Canada, Pierre Elliott Trudeau

Instead of "significant"historical landmarks, Ānandamayī Mā's *lilā* from 1932 to the present constitutes an unending procession of religious festivals, *kīrtana*s and *satsaṅga*s (religious gatherings). And the bliss-permeated Mother continues to roam all over Northern India surrounded by some of Her closest followers and eagerly awaited by thousands of devotees who hope to benefit from Her presence. Of course, some of those who used to accompany the

Ānandamayī Mā with her mother Didimā

Mother are no longer with Her. In 1937 Bhāijī joined Ānandamayī Mā on a pilgrimage to Mount Kailāsh, the mythical abode of Lord Śiva. On the way Bhāijī was suddenly overcome by an urge for complete renunciation. Ānandamayī Mā spontaneously uttered *mantra*s accompanying *saṁnyāsa*[25] initiation and bestowed upon him the monastic name Swami Mounananda Parvat. A few days following his initiation he contracted a fever and died in Almora with the words "Mā, Mā" on his lips. Bholānāth died of small pox in 1938. Two years earlier, in 1936, Ānandamayī Mā's father had passed on. His wife, Didimā, became a renunciant under the name of Swami Muktananda Giri in 1939. Since Ānandamayī Mā does not consider Herself a *guru*, She frequently asked Her mother to initiate devotees. Indefatigably Didimā served at her daughter's side until her death at the age of ninety-three, on August 8th, 1970.

[25] According to the ancient Hindu system, *saṁnyāsa* is the last stage of human life, in which a man has to renounce his family, possessions, caste, social position, etc. and surrender himself to the divine.

Since the number of Ānandamayī Mā's followers had tremendously increased over the years and new *āśram*s had sprung up across northern and central India, a regular organization was needed for administrative purposes. In February, 1950, the Shree Shree Anandamayee Sangha was established in Vārāṇasi with the following objectives: (1) to promote methods aiming at Self-realization, (2) to start centers for practicing *sādhanā*, (3) to organize religious functions, (4) to give free medical relief to deserving persons and provide financial and medical assistance to *sādhu*s (renunciants) and *brahmacāri*s (celibate students). The bliss-permeated Mother is in no way involved in the management or control of the Shree Shree Anandamayee Sangha. Its governing body consists of forty-one members while the day-to-day activities are supervised by an executive council of ten. Contributions from laymen are its only source of revenue. The Sangha has established two institutions in which a balanced spiritual, mental, and physical education is provided for boys and girls separately. Since 1952, a quarterly journal, *Ananda Vārtā*, has been published, in Bengali, Hindi, and English. In its pages one can find not only Ānandamayī Mā's teaching and news about Her but also spiritually uplifting articles on all religions. In 1965 a modern hospital was founded in Vārāṇasi providing free treatment for destitute persons.

Although Ānandamayī Mā has shown relatively little concern for institutions devoted to

Ānandamayī Mā at the Vārāṇasi *āśram*

man's material welfare, She did attend the opening of the hospital and gave Her blessings to its functioning. The institution for which She personally is responsible, however, is the annual *Samyam Vrata*s (vow of self-restraint, self-control), started in 1952. She is well aware of the fact that modern men, even in India, are deeply enmeshed in worldly activities and rarely willing to live a life of total renunciation. Knowing that "the world is too much with us," She wants the lay devotees to abandon worldly living for at least one week each year and to devote that time entirely to spiritual pursuits. The *Samyam Vrata*s take place each year in a different location, either in *āśram*s or on grounds provided for that purpose by wealthy devotees. Participants vow to fast except for one light meal a day and to abstain from quarrelling, gossiping, smoking, drinking tea and coffee (not to speak of alcohol), and sex during that week. Everyone lives in utmost simplicity, sometimes in tents. Pandits and *mahātmā*s address the "renunciants for a week" during the day. At night Ānandamayī Mā holds *satsaṅga* for about an hour. Some time is spent in *kīrtana* and collective meditation. Several hundred people, including a few westerners, attend the *Samyam Vrata*s as a rule. One devotee appropriately called the *Samyam Vrata*s "spiritual training grounds." They may be regarded as beacons at a time when the majority of men are enveloped in a darkness created by their material-mindedness. The bliss-permeated Mother considers them building blocs for a new society, a society whose primary concern is not the accumulation of material wealth but God-realization.

By urging mankind to renounce the world for one week, Ānandamayī Mā is asking them to practice only an infinitesimal fraction of that renunciation which has been Her way of life for half a century. She has no home and in spite of Her advanced age continues to be "a bird on the wing." All the gifts that are showered upon Her leave Her indifferent and are often immediately distributed to others.

At the time of writing the bliss-permeated Mother is in Her seventy-seventh year. Naturally, time has left its mark on Her body. Her health leaves much to be desired from a normal worldly "human" point of view. Ānandamayī Mā, however, remains undisturbed: "For this body there is no cause whatever for inconvenience or discomfort. This (ill-health) is also

a fine play. This body observes in minute detail what is taking place in its every nerve and vein…. For this body, everything without exception is but a play…. Whatever be the *kheyāla* at any particular moment, according to that, things may happen." So, in sickness or health She goes on, a constant reminder to all of us that we too should strive to attain a state beyond duality where no physical suffering can touch us.

Editor's Postscript

Ānandamayī Mā lived on for nine years after the time of Professor Lipski's writing, continuing all the while to radiate divine bliss for the benefit of humanity. She "became unmanifest" on August 26th, 1982, at the age of eighty-six, and was buried in her *āśram* in Kankhal near the banks of the Ganges. During her funeral endless streams of people from all walks of life came to pay homage to their spiritual mother. "One could see them coming as far as the eye could see. They came in cars, rickshaws, and on foot."[26] Twenty-five years have now elapsed since Mā's passing from this world, yet her blissful presence continues to be felt by countless devotees and admirers across the world. This should not surprise us, for, "Who goes away—who else is it that arrives? What is the distinction between life and death? One who passes away, in fact, merges into the One who is ever-existent." Ānandamayī Mā, the bliss-permeated Mother, is indeed ever-existent.

---

[26] *India Today*, September 4th.

Ānandamayī Mā's *āśram* at New Delhi

Ānandamayī Mā's Samādhi Mandir (burial shrine) at Kankhal

CHAPTER II
Personality and Teachings

How is one to deal with the personality of someone who defies all categorization, so dear to the western analytic mind? Her devotees to this day wonder who She really is. Learned disquisitions have been written analyzing various possibilities. Is She a God-intoxicated mystic? Is She an *avatāra*? Is She the Absolute Itself? Is She a manifestation of the Divine Mother? The Italian devotee Miriam Orr concludes: "Mother is not a human being like all the others. She is divine light clad in a human form." No attempt will be made in this study to decide who the bliss-permeated Mother really is. It may be useful though to elaborate on the Mother aspect of Ānandamayī Mā. While in the west God is thought of as Father, in India many revere the Divine in the form of the Mother. In Bengal especially Mother Kālī or Mother Durgā have been venerated since ancient times. Undoubtedly Ānandamayī Mā possesses a specific motherly appeal. Some of Her closest devotees who had lost their own mother found that Ānandamayī Mā fulfilled their need for a mother, but in a way no ordinary human being would be able to do.

Can we obtain a clue to Her identity from the bliss-permeated Mother Herself? Naturally She has been frequently asked to reveal Herself. At one occasion She stated: "From your worldly standpoint this body belongs to East Bengal and is a *brāhman* by caste; but if you think apart from these artificial distinctions, you will understand that this body is one of the members of one human family." If we consider that all verbal expressions are by their very nature limited, the closest approximation to truth about Ānandamayī Mā seems to be contained in Her answer: "Well, I am what you consider me to be, not more, not less." Or: "This body is like

a musical instrument; what you hear depends upon how you play it." Is it not rather striking that although many a skilled photographer has tried his hand at taking Her picture, each photograph has turned out distinctly different. One is tempted to conclude that we are witnessing in Her "person" the infinitely varying aspects of the cosmos. Under those circumstances, our vision of Ānandamayī Mā will even fall short of the description rendered by the legendary six blind boys who washed different parts of an elephant's body and produced six distinct accounts of how the elephant looks. It will depend upon our state of consciousness, to what extent we shall be able to fathom the phenomenon called Ānandamayī Mā.

There seems to be general agreement that She does not exhibit what is normally considered ego-consciousness. No personal likes or dislikes, cravings or aversions are apparent. At no time did She have to face the agonizing struggles, conflicts, temptations, and doubts occurring in the lives of even the greatest saints. She is totally devoid of fear and anger. Whenever She displays moods it is clear that She is acting in that manner to bring home a certain point, to teach a lesson. Instead of being the captive of common human motivations and impulses, She follows what She terms *kheyāla*. Ordinarily it means spontaneous action, or even caprice, but the way Ānandamayī Mā employs it to explain Her own actions and behavior as well as that of God or the Absolute, it is best translated as "divine Will," with the implication that it is not subject to the normal cause and effect process. It is thus entirely free from any conditioning. Ānandamayī Mā's "decisions" to stay in one place or another, to cure one person but not another, Her reaction to various *darśana* seekers with kindness, severity, indifference, or attentiveness, are all explained by Her as the result of *kheyāla*. For example, She visited Dr. Gopinath Kaviraj in June, 1961, while he was lying in a hospital in Bombay. On the way out She had the *kheyāla* to stop at the bed of a Muslim patient who was dying from cancer. She stroked all over his body blessing him. Obviously there were many other deathly sick patients, but Her *kheyāla* singled him out. Once She stunned Her devotees by greeting with laughter a disciple who had just suffered the loss of his wife. Offended by Her seemingly callous attitude, he asked Her for the cause of Her merriment. "Pitājī" (an endearment of father), She replied, "There is one less barrier between you and God." On the other hand, Ānandamayī Mā can act kindly beyond human comprehension. A young man had terribly misbehaved while staying in one of Her *āśram*s. He was most egotistic and stubborn, driving the other *āśram* inmates to desperation. They finally told Ānandamayī Mā that he ought to be expelled from the *āśram*. But She replied: "When nobody wants such a poor and hapless boy, don't you think that he needs me most? Will it do you and the world any good if this perverse young man is allowed to rot in the mire?" The young misfit stayed and in time became one of Her finest devotees.

Ānandamayī Mā dressed as Kṛṣṇa

As Her name indicates, She is considered the very incarnation of bliss. Even now, although She is advanced in years, Her pealing laughter is infectious. Seeing Her one realizes the truth proclaimed by the *Taittirīya Upaniṣad*: "From joy springs the universe." Countless are the humorous stories and incidents from Her life which She enjoys telling in the intimate circle of Her close devotees. Once some devotees dressed Her as the boy Kṛṣṇa and She became identified with the youthful prank-loving god. She is completely in tune with nature. During a boat trip to Cox Bazar in East Bengal, a tremendous storm erupted. Most passengers were panicky with fear, but Ānandamayī Mā enjoyed the spectacle. Looking at the tossing waves She remarked: "Listen to the uninterrupted *kīrtana* that is going on over there." Just as does Lord Śiva in the form of *Naṭarāja*, the Cosmic Dancer, She experiences the thrill of the cosmic play, be it ever so destructive. It is true that occasionally She shows signs of exhaustion, especially after a celebration in Calcutta, where thousands upon thousands of devotees pass by Her, offering garlands to Her, which She returns to them with a blessing. There are times when She experiences sickness, but, as has been pointed out earlier, She accepts all bodily discomfort with equanimity. Being anchored in the one Reality, why should She reject this essential aspect of delusive manifestation? It too gives Her joy, She avers. Once, after She had been seriously ill in August, 1929, She explained: "This body moves in tune with nature, its natural course must have somehow been thwarted in its normal functioning," indicating that Her devotees had attempted to interfere with Her *kheyāla*.

Her followers claim that She is continuously in the highest state of *samādhi*. Even as She looks at you, you are aware of the fact that She is with you and yet far beyond you; that She has that dual vision encompassing the manifest and the transcendent. In Her presence one feels as though mentally stripped naked. There is no point in trying to hide anything. As uncomfortable as this may appear to be, it is tempered by the realization that Ānandamayī Mā understands all and does not condemn anyone, for from Her point of view you are, above all, a soul, possibly greatly tarnished by egoistic tendencies, but still a soul. Being in Her presence produces a consciousness of one's imperfections as well as an extreme feeling of serenity. Even a beginner on the spiritual path will sense that he is in intimate contact with the Divine, especially if he has the privilege to be present during one of those occasions when She chants, to the accompaniment of a harmonium, either "*He Bhagavān!* (O, Lord!)," or "*Satyam, jñānam, anantam, Brahma* (Truth, wisdom, infinite, Absolute)." Her voice has remained youthful even though Her body is aging. Her chanting sweeps

Ānandamayī Mā at a *kirtana* (singing of devotional songs)

49

aside all earthly attachments, and, at least temporarily, one feels in tune with the One. The quintessence of Her being is summed up in the statement: "The most remarkable characteristic of Mā Ānandamayī... is to awaken or intensify the keen desire for the spiritual life in all who approach Her."

While Ānandamayī Mā refuses to be considered a *guru*, She cannot escape being constantly approached for spiritual guidance. For all practical purposes She does have disciples, even though they may not have received formal initiation from Her. And She is ever ready to teach by Her very being, by Her actions, and by direct counseling. Warning people not to depend on book learning, She teaches in a simple, homely language, often by means of parables, just as did Ramakrishna. She is particularly fond of punning, for which Bengali is well suited. Thus *Vedānta* (monistic Indian philosophy) means

bheda anta (end of difference); where Rāma (God) is, there is *ārāma* (rest); where Rāma is not, there is *byārāmā* (discomfort, disease); desire (*vāsanā*) is where God does not dwell (*vāsa nā*); *sādhanā* has to be practiced to discover *svā dhana* (one's own wealth).[1] Frequently She does not offer specific advice. Instead She points out various ways of viewing a problem. For instance, someone asked Her whether it was proper for him to engage in a suit, in view of the fact that he had been cheated in a business deal. In reply, She stated that one could argue that one must go to court to teach the culprit a lesson and to keep him from further crime. On the other hand, who is really cheating? "Are not all forms, all beings manifestations of Him? What I have been deprived of was evidently not my due. It is

---

[1] In Bengali *sādhanā* and *svā dhana* have the almost identical pronunciation.

God who has taken it from me." Another way of looking at the problem is that through generosity and forgiveness one might bring about a transformation in the criminal. Or one might refrain from going to court, considering it sufficient punishment that the villain had caused bad *karma*[2] for himself. Finally, one could reason that one would not go to court if the wrongdoer were one's own brother. "Whichever of these points of view appeals to you, according to it you should act."

When someone complained to Ānandamayī Mā about Her unwillingness to give clear-cut answers to problems, She retorted: "At least you have understood that there is a state where problems are no longer settled in any particular way…no solution is ever conclusive.… The resolution of a problem arrived at by the mind must of necessity be from a particular point of view; consequently there will be room for contradiction, since your solution represents but one aspect." Only by transcending the region of multifacedness can one arrive at *the* one solution.

Ānandamayī Mā uses every possible occasion to teach. At Her *āśram* in Solon, for instance, the entrance is guarded by two wooden tigers. They have been so realistically painted that they appear as though they are on the verge of pouncing upon any potential prey. Once when a dog came to the *āśram* to beg for food, Ānandamayī Mā placed some food close to the wooden tigers. The dog obviously was in a quandary, he was eager to eat the food but fear of the tigers kept him from touching it. Ānandamayī Mā thereupon jokingly remarked that the dog found himself in the position of most human beings who are held captive by their imaginary fears.

Directly or indirectly Ānandamayī Mā works on those who have entrusted their lives to Her guidance to rid themselves of imperfections. Vijayānanda (Dr. Weintrob) relates that he had

shown undue concern about finding seating accommodations for himself during their frequent travels—anyone knowing how overcrowded Indian trains are will sympathize with his weakness. Craving for material comforts, however, is an obstacle to spiritual advancement. Once Vijayānanda had just figured out exactly how he could obtain for himself a desirable seat and had taken up an advantageous position on the station platform. His shrewd calculation was unfortunately upset by Ānandamayī Mā. When the train pulled into the station, She asked him to take care of a big assortment of baggage and to see to it that it be safely put on the train. It was a drastic lesson in overcoming selfishness. Apparently he learnt that lesson quickly, for, as a "reward," Ānandamayī Mā saw to it that he did get a suitable seat. Vijayānanda also tells us that the bliss-permeated Mother can be most persistent in pointing out over and over again specific shortcomings of Her devotees, such

---

[2] Action, the result of action, as well as the law of cause and effect by which actions inevitably bear their fruit.

as loss of temper, quarrelsomeness, or tendency to gossip, right in front of other devotees. Vijayānanda relates that he had used intemperate language towards one of the *āśram* inmates in Ma's presence. He almost immediately re-

gretted his loss of self-control and asked Her forgiveness in private, hoping that this obviously minor matter would thereby be laid at rest. However, Ānandamayī Mā questioned all those concerned in the incident in a most elaborate manner, dwelling on it for what seemed an un-due amount of time. Later Vijayānanda came to understand that it was Her method to eradicate thoroughly whatever shortcoming may prove a hindrance in one's spiritual progress. By pay-ing exceptional attention to his minor failing and examining it in detail, She made him aware of the underlying cause for his flare-up, some pent-up emotion. Before long he was able to overcome this imperfection.

Like the Divine Mother She can be exceed-ingly compassionate at one time and seemingly cruel at another, whatever approach is deemed necessary to free Her charges from delusion. Her teaching is always adjusted to the needs of the individual and varies in accordance with his or her religious background. It does not matter whether one is a monist, dualist, Muslim, Bud-dhist, or Christian. Ānandamayī Mā has the ability to attune Herself to the particular reli-gious point of view and the level of understand-ing of those who consult Her. Vijayānanda ob-serves: "A *vedāntist*, for example, when talking to Mother for the first time, will feel convinced that She is a pure *advaita* (non-dualist) *vedāntin*; a *śākta* (worshipper of the Divine Mother) may very likely say that She is an incarnation of the Divine Mother, advocating the cult of *śakti* (di-vine energy personified as feminine; the Divine Mother); while a *vaiṣṇava* will see in Her a great *bhakta* (follower of the devotional path). It is only after having known Her fairly closely and for a long time that one becomes aware of Her innumerable facets." Arnaud Desjardins reported that Ānandamayī Mā brought him closer to Christ. Buddhists, Sikhs, and Muslims find that She strengthens their faith in their respective beliefs. The gist of Ānandamayī Mā's message is that only One (God, *Brahman*) truly exists: "The One who is the Eternal, the *Ātman* (true Self), He Himself is the traveler on the path of Immortality. He is all in all, He alone is." Everything else is nothing but an elabora-tion of this statement, just a commentary. Thus, in the ultimate sense, one may consider Her a monist, provided one understands that dualism is a facet of monism, for it is the One that seeks expression in infinite varieties of forms, ways, and events. It is the One that is engaged in the *līlā* of creation, preservation, and destruction. It is the One that is deeply involved in every aspect of the *līlā* and yet is beyond the *līlā*. Actually He (the One) plays hide and seek with Himself. Absolute oneness makes a *līlā* impos-sible. So, to enjoy the *līlā*, the One has created the veil of separateness (*māyā*) as a disguise, but we must not forget that He Himself is also the disguise. He is disguised as manifoldness, vari-ety, relativity. Often Ānandamayī Mā uses the analogy of water or the ocean to explain how the One can have different aspects. By varying the temperature, one can turn water into ice or steam, without changing its essential nature. Similarly, stormy weather can temporarily di-vide an ocean into individual waves but when calm returns, the waves merge into the ocean. All come from One and return to One.

To give an illustration of God's game of hide and seek, Ānandamayī Mā tells the fol-lowing story. A wealthy merchant once went on a business trip. A thief in the disguise of a busi-nessman joined him, intent upon robbing him at the earliest suitable occasion. Every morning, before leaving the inn in which they happened to have put up for the night, the merchant would count his money quite openly and then put it into his pocket. At night the merchant went to sleep seemingly without suspicion. While he was asleep the thief would frantically search through all the belongings of the mer-chant without being able to find the money. Af-ter several nights of frustrating searching, the thief finally in resignation confessed to the mer-chant his true intention and pleaded with him to tell him how he was able to hide his money so successfully. The merchant replied casually: "I knew from the beginning what you were up to. So, every night I placed the money under your pillow. I could safely sleep, knowing fully well that that would be the one place where you would never look." And Ānandamayī Mā comments: "God is within everyone, but man goes out in search of Him. This is what constitutes God's play and God's creation."

Unity in variety also applies to the religious realm. Just as individual human beings have been created with various tendencies, abilities, temperaments, so religious paths have come about in response to different religious needs. Men may dispute which is the ideal path, but when the goal of Oneness is reached, all quarrelling ceases, for quarrelling presupposes alternatives, distinctions. Holding such a view Ānandamayī Mā, while showing utmost respect for Christianity, unequivocally rejects Christianity's claim to the one true religion. How dare anyone assume that the *infinite* Lord would provide only one path of salvation.

Irrespective of which religious path one embraces, the aim of religion must be to pierce through the veil of delusion to discover the underlying Oneness, and ultimately to merge with the One. This is the foremost, nay, the only duty of man. This is what distinguishes man from all other creatures: "…it is man's duty to bear in mind that he exists for God alone—for His service and for the realization of Him." Finding the One is the cure-all for all worldly sufferings and human imperfections. For how is it possible to show hostility towards anyone or anything when one knows that all beings and all things are interrelated and essentially one. Then and only then does it become possible to accept, even welcome all of life's experiences, be they ever so painful. It must have been this unitary view that enabled St. Francis to welcome sickness and death, to feel kinship with all life including Brother Fire and Sister Sun.

Why the many exist and why this *līlā* is going on cannot really be explained in finite terms. The One who is beyond time and space is equally beyond cause and effect which are aspects of delusion. Thus the question "why?" is itself a facet of *māyā*. The mind which operates on the basis of time and space, cause and effect, is in no way able to grasp ultimate Reality. Consequently, only when one has personally experienced Oneness, i.e. transcended multiplicity, will one be able to know ultimate Truth, a truth that is beyond the "why." This world is a world of contradictions and no sense can be made of it as long as one is involved in it. But it is our good fortune that the One who has created the veil

of delusion has also provided us with the ways and means to annihilate delusion. And it is delusion itself that eventually becomes the means for overcoming delusion.

Being deluded, man believes that this world of duality is real, and that he can find happiness in it. But the world has been so constructed that it cannot provide real i.e., lasting happiness. The word world (*jagat*, movement) gives the clue to its nature. It is constant movement, perpetual change, coming and going, health and sickness, fame and disgrace, richness and poverty, birth and death. No permanent contentment, no peace "that passeth understanding" can be expected in this world. Man must realize that it is not his true home. "When one resides in a country not one's own, how can one possibly evade the hardships that are a foreigner's lot? Your Motherland is where there is no question of distress and sorrow, of violence and hatred, of estrangement, neither of the opposites of light and darkness." Being an alien, a visitor, man must not tarry here unduly. As long as he in his

ignorance believes that he can find happiness here, whether in the form of fame, richness, power, or human love, he will, upon death, have to return to this world for further lessons. His earthly attachments will automatically provide him with a "return ticket" as Ānandmayī Mā so fittingly describes it.

Since Ānandamayī Mā urges man to start upon the return trip to the One, does She imply that man has free will successfully to undertake the journey by his own efforts? As we well know, theologians across the centuries have disputed this thorny question. She makes it clear that there is a subtle interrelationship between free will and grace, free will being in the ultimate sense a part of grace, as contradictory as this may sound. Thus She states: "Verily, everything in the world is achieved by will-power. If by determination and patience someone can translate his ideal into life, his actions will be inspired. Such a worker is backed by divine power." As long as we are in ignorance, we are seemingly free in minor matters only. Our

weaknesses, our inadequacies bind us. We are the slaves of our moods, cravings, and impulses. Ānandamayī Mā likens the average man's freedom to that of a cow which is tied by a rope to a post. Within the limits of the rope she has freedom. But, of course, were the cow able to break loose from the rope, she would gain complete freedom. Similarly, the person who makes the right spiritual effort can cut thereby the rope of delusion that binds him to the finite world of pseudo-happiness and attain freedom.

Over and over again Ānandamayī Mā states: "All that occurs, good or bad,—if it was predestined to happen—comes about through the mysterious working together of certain forces," or "Whatever happens was destined to happen." The bliss-permeated Mother is, however, by no means a strict predestinarian. The law of *karma* is not the only factor to be considered, for God is not bound by any laws. His free will prevails over man's seemingly free will. To illustrate this point She uses the following analogy. A man who has planted flowers in his garden may decide to plant fruit-trees instead. He will obviously have to remove the flowers to make room for the fruit-trees. In like manner, but on a vaster scale, God, the great gardener, rearranges the universe, according to His design. She does not elaborate upon God's design except to indicate that it is beneficial for man's spiritual development, for the very nature of God is compassion. Because God is compassionate, man can appeal to Him in prayer. It is here where grace comes in. In fact, Ānandamayī Mā speaks of two types of grace. Normally grace operates even within the law of *karma*. As will be pointed out in detail in connection with the discussion of *sādhanā*, *karma* operates in a way that even the greatest sinner will eventually "decide" to embark upon the road to liberation. This implies that grace is built into the very mechanism of the universe. It is for this reason that Ānandamayī Mā considers all actions, all experiences beneficial. But in addition to universal grace there is special grace. Through grace, God can wipe out entirely the karmic debts (consequences) of those who appeal to Him sincerely and with utmost devotion. They can be lifted by Him to that transcendent sphere where *karma* does not operate. While so much of Hindu religious thought is concerned with *karma* and ways of avoiding rebirth into this valley of tears, the message of Ānandamayī Mā emphasizes the fact that *karma* and rebirth are nothing but aspects of delusion. Therefore, Ānandamayī Mā

discourages people from trying to discover what they might have been in previous incarnations, deeming such inquiry futile, a waste of time: "…when you can visualize five hundred of your former births, you are still limited by number—for there is so very much more than this!… In reality there is no question of time and out of time, of day and night, of before and after; so long as you remain enslaved by time there will be birth and death. Actually there is no such thing. It is true that at some stage the memory of previous lives will certainly occur; on the other hand, what is the significance of before and after, since 'I exist throughout eternity.'"

To understand Ānandamayī Mā's views about *karma* and reincarnation, it is essential to keep in mind that She constantly shifts to and fro between the transcendent and the manifest realm. While She contends that *karma* has no ultimate reality, She expounds the working of *karma* on the level of time and space. To illustrate that ordinarily man cannot escape from destiny, i.e., reaping the fruits of his *karma*, She narrated the following story. The wife and children of a learned *brāhman* had been killed by a poisonous snake. Deeply distressed the *brāhman* went in pursuit of the snake and finally located it in a nearby forest. As he approached the murderous reptile, it turned into a buffalo. Subsequently the buffalo pounced upon another buffalo and killed him. Immediately thereafter the killer buffalo transformed himself into a beautiful young girl. Two men happened to pass by. Both instantaneously fell in love with the maiden and started to fight with each other over her. When one of them was fatally wounded, the maiden walked off nonchalantly. The *brāhman* who had watched the various transformations and the tragic killings finally caught up with the girl and, deeply mystified, asked her who she really was. "I am destiny," she retorted. When he inquired what destiny was in store for him, she informed him that he would die through drowning, whereupon she disappeared. The *brāhman* was determined to defy destiny.

Since he had lost his family, he had no desire to remain any longer in his home, which reminded him of a happiness that no longer existed. He started searching for a new place to settle—a place remote from lakes, rivers, or oceans. At long last he came to an apparently ideal location. There he made the acquaintance of a wealthy man who upon hearing about his sad experience invited him to live in his home, to be part of his family. In return he was to become the teacher of the rich man's only son. The son became exceedingly fond of him and when he grew up and got married, he asked his teacher to stay with him and to become the teacher of

his future son. In due course a son was born and when he was old enough he received lessons from the *brāhman*. One day the family decided to make a pilgrimage to the Ganges, India's most sacred river. Naturally the *brāhman* was asked to accompany the family. At first he resisted the family's pleading. When he revealed to them the reason why he was reluctant to participate in the pilgrimage and to bathe in the holy Ganges, they reassured him that they would have a special enclosed bathing area constructed for him and their son. In order not to offend them and especially his beloved pupil, he then agreed to come along. As soon as the *brāhman* and the

The ghat on the Ganges of the Kali temple at Calcutta

The Manikarnika ghat (the "burning" ghat) on the Ganges at Vārāṇasi

boy entered the enclosed bathing area, the boy changed into a crocodile, seized the *brāhman*, broke through the fence, and carried him towards the open river. Before drowning him, he addressed the *brāhman*: "Don't you recognize me? I am destiny."

Another story further reinforces the point that none can resist destiny. An old man had died in a village far from the Ganges. His family, who were very devout, wanted him to be cremated at the Ganges—the most auspicious site for ending life. The corpse was consequently to be transported to the Ganges by specially hired carriers. Since they were unable to make the trip in one day, the carriers stopped in a village at nightfall and took rest in an inn. It so happened that in that village an extremely pious but poor and lonely old woman was on the point of dying. Her greatest yearning had been to be cremated at the Ganges, but since she had no close relatives it seemed that her desire would go unfulfilled. When she found out about the bier-carriers, it flashed through her mind that

this was her chance to attain her goal. Strength surged into her and with utmost determination she managed to remove the corpse from the bier while the carriers were asleep and placed herself on the bier instead. The carriers awoke before dawn and continued the journey in darkness, not noticing the change. The moment they reached the Ganges, the old woman died. Upon arrival at the cremation grounds, the carriers discovered that they had carried the wrong corpse. By that time it was too late to correct the "error." The old woman was cremated as she had so ardently hoped for. The other body was found later, already substantially decomposed. Destiny had had its way: "Whatever is due to anyone, anywhere, God will bring it about by a combination of circumstances."

Given Ānandamayī Mā's view concerning destiny, it is not surprising that She urges man to accept all circumstances, all vicissitudes of life as coming from Him. Adverse conditions are not sent to torture us, but to lead us towards total liberation. Probably, of all "adverse" condi-

of his true home. "Happiness that depends on anything, be it a person, money, comforts, and so forth cannot endure....God alone can give lasting contentment." Ānandamayī Mā also warns Her devotees not to indulge in excessive mourning at the time of bereavement, because this can be an obstacle to the spiritual progress of both the deceased and the survivor. The soul of the deceased is being kept earthbound by the thoughts of the mourner, while the survivor increases his matter-attachment. He should also remember that the *Ātmā* (Self) does not die, and that the other person's and his *Ātmā* are one. Above all, man should not cry for the loss of a body but rather cry for God. Of course, it is human to shed tears at the death of a loved one but the loss must not paralyze one's vitality: "It is man's duty to remain steady and calm under all circumstances, and to pray only for the welfare of the soul."

Once a male devotee asked Ānandamayī Mā whether by committing suicide upon the death of his beloved wife he would be able to join her. In the strongest possible terms She condemned suicide: "To whom belongs the body that you speak of destroying? Is this the way a human being talks? For shame!" And She added that suicide is nothing but a foolish attempt to escape from harvesting one's *karma*. It only further retards spiritual progress. However, She does not consider that a woman who had become *satī* (literally "chaste woman"), i.e. a widow who had burnt herself on her husband's funeral pyre, had thereby committed suicide. As far as Ānandamayī Mā was concerned, *satī* was a ritual death, a confirmation of a wife's unconditional loyalty to her husband and an expression of true chastity. "A real *satī* has to be completely steady in mind and body. If, entering the fire she suffers, she cannot be called a *satī*." If thus her conduct in life has been totally unblemished, she will be fearless at the time of immolation. In this connection Ānandamayī Mā tells about one of Her ancestors who put one of her fingers into the flame of a candle to test whether

tions, death is the one which man finds most difficult to accept. It is therefore understandable that devotees frequently come to Ānandamayī Mā when they have suffered the loss of a dear one. A couple who had recently lost their child visited Ānandamayī Mā in Her *āśram* at Hardwar and wanted to know the significance of premature death. The bliss-permeated Mother replied: "Everything happens according to one's *karma*. It was your *karma* to serve your son for a few years, and his *karma* to accept your service. When it was over, God took him away. It is all God's play. Some flowers fall off without bearing fruit...." An American lady told Ānandamayī Mā that she had lost her husband with whom she had been exceedingly happily married. His death made life meaningless for her. In reply Ānandamayī Mā explained to her that all human attachments eventually have to be given up. God does not want man to have any worldly fetters. When man becomes too engrossed in the world of delusion, the objects of his attachment are withdrawn from him, to remind him

she would be able to endure the pain of being burnt. She experienced no pain. Subsequently she ascended her husband's funeral pyre, lay down and remained completely motionless while the flames consumed her body. Westerners will probably be repelled by this story and by Ānandamayī Mā's approval of *satī*. From Her point of view the motive is all-important. The true *satī* is not escaping from life but is fulfilling her duty according to the *dharma* (right way of living) prevailing within her cultural milieu at that time. She is acting selflessly and shows that she is unattached to the delusive body. It must be emphasized that Ānandamayī Mā does not advocate *satī* in this present age.

If we want truly to understand Ānandamayī Mā's attitude towards death, we must constantly remind ourselves that our modern western view of death as man's enemy is alien to Her. "The pilgrim on the path of immortality never contemplates death. By meditation on the Immortal the fear of death recedes far away—remember this! In the measure that your contemplation of the One becomes uninterrupted, you will advance towards full, unbroken realization."

Man's spiritual evolution is greatly affected by the thought he harbors at the time of death. "Just as a leech does not leave its place without hooking on to something else, so the soul at the time of leaving the body hooks on to some kind of new existence according to the state of mind of the dying person." Let no one conclude, however, that he can live according to his whims, indulging in sense pleasures oblivious of God, and that at the moment of death he will be able to catapult himself into the divine presence by thinking the right thoughts. This is a miscalculation, for man is a creature of habit and therefore at death his mind will dwell on those thoughts that have occupied him most during his life.

To substantiate this point Ānandamayī Mā told of a greedy old woman, an oil vendor, who lay upon her death bed. All her life she had sold oil in the bazaar. At no time had she granted anyone credit, and never had she given away even the smallest quantity of oil. When beggars asked her for oil, she used to reply: "Not a drop will I give, not a drop." While she was on the verge of dying, her relatives, concerned about her spiritual welfare, tried to make her repeat "Rāma" or "Kṛṣṇa," but all she was capable of uttering was: "Not a drop will I give, not a drop." This had become her *mantra*.

The foregoing account is meant to show that man's day-to-day thoughts and activities throughout his life determine his state of consciousness and his spiritual destiny. It is for this reason that Ānandamayī Mā urges Her devotees to be ever concentrated on God, to practice the divine presence, to engage in *sādhanā*. In one sense everyone is practicing *sādhanā*, for,

as was pointed out in the discussion of grace, all human beings are subject to grace, and all activities ultimately lead towards God. But one should not take too much comfort from this thought, for there are direct roads as well as detours, and some roads are smoother than others. The vast majority of human beings are not consciously traveling anywhere. Nor are they even aware of the fact that they ought to seek God-realization. Completely caught up in delusion, they focus all their attention on the material world. But the world is so constituted that it cannot provide lasting contentment. Because man has within him a drive for perfection, he is bound to be frustrated in an imperfect world. Man is attracted to material pleasures initially because they are tangible. His essential nature, however, is spirit and spirit cannot be satisfied with material food. The starvation of the spirit is not noticeable at first. Only when material objects have disappointed him, does he begin consciously to seek in a non-material direction and thus begins deliberately his *sādhanā*. The great stimulant to spiritual endeavor is pain and suffering, man's true friends, according to Ānandamayī Mā: "Remember, one is born to experience various kinds of joys and sorrows according to one's desire. For the time being, God comes to you in the disguise of suffering. He is purifying you in this manner. The suffering is for your own best. A mother gives a slap to her beloved child for its own good, in order to keep it on the right path. When a fond mother gives her baby a bath, the child may scream desperately, yet the mother will not let the baby go until she has thoroughly washed and scrubbed him...." Thus suffering is a necessity, a means of purification, and a means of instilling ardor into man to seek God, the only source of happiness. If man only knew that God is most relishable. But just as someone who has never eaten a *rasagulla* (Bengali sweet), cannot imagine its sweetness, man who has not experienced the Divine, cannot know the supreme bliss of God's presence.

To become aware of God's presence and ultimately become one with Him, one has to engage in *sādhanā*. This requires effort at first, but success is not attained until *sādhanā* has become effortless. The beginner on the path will have to exert himself, use all his will-power to overcome the pull of the world. Ānandamayī Mā likens *sādhanā* to a bitter pill prescribed by the doctor for our cure. Similarly, spiritual effort appears unpleasant initially. Gross pleasures of the senses are easily accessible; the more subtle joys of the spirit can only be attained after a complete redirection of our energies, a refocusing of our attention, and a conquest of habits established over many lives. Yet there is no alternative, the bitter pill of *sādhanā* has to be swallowed, if one wants to be healed from suffering. When steady effort has resulted in the first glimpses of God's bliss, one's enthusiasm becomes aroused. Worldly attractions decrease as God's magnetic pull is being felt, and in the end we approach effortlessly the divine goal: "To realize God means to realize one's Self. How can there be strain while engaging in the essential thing for oneself?" As we identify with our true Self, delusive selfishness drops off. We find freedom in God. Unfortunately, many of us delay swallowing the medicine. When old age comes we lament: "Eventide has come and life is ebbing away. O Lord, have mercy upon me and take me across." But rarely can we at that stage muster that amount of energy required to attract the divine grace.

In general, one's desire for God is the most important element for a successful *sādhanā*. We must crave for God "with all our heart, all our mind, and all our soul." We must yearn for God as the shipwrecked sailor longs for the shore. We must be as intent in our search for God as the businessman is upon financial success. All other duties must be subordinated to *sādhanā*.

"Infinite are the *sādhanā*s...." There are no hard and fast rules. The path most suitable for one person may in no way be ideal for someone else. Mātājī places special importance

on repetition of the divine name, "keeping one's mouth sweet," as She sometimes calls it.[3] The bliss-permeated Mother also urges Her devotees to listen to religious talks by *mahātmā*s, to study sacred writings, to engage in *kīrtana*, always keeping in mind that all techniques are meant to acquaint man with God until such time that God becomes an ever-present reality, that He,

the One is perceived behind all manifestations. Whether one calls Him Rāma, Kṛṣṇa, Christ, or Buddha is immaterial. Once while Ānandamayī Mā was walking through a village, the local inhabitants asked Her which name of God they ought to invoke. Ānandamayī Mā raised three fingers of Her right hand and, pointing to each of them said: "This is Rāma, this Kṛṣṇa, this Śiva. Now catch hold of one!" As far as *hathayoga* (the practice of bodily postures) is concerned, Ānandamayī Mā points out that normally its only goal is physical agility, which

[3] One not too perceptive devotee had taken Her advice literally and had eaten sugar candy daily. After a year's "practice" he complained that he had not yet attained God-realization!

by itself is of little value. If one practices it, however, to attain stillness of the body, in order to perceive the Divine better, then *hathayoga* is beneficial.[4]

Perfoming *pūjā* at the bank of the Ganges in Hrishikesh

When asked whether formal worship (*pūjā*) is necessary for the attainment of Self-realization, Ānandamayī Mā often emphasizes the fact that ritual rightly applied is often of great help when one practices *sādhanā*. Through regular worship one cultivates devotion, one establishes an intimate relationship with Him whom one worships. Loving devotion will lead to a tangi-

[4] See also pp. 100-101 (in chapter 3).

ble experience of the divine presence. There will subsequently come a time, provided one continues ardently one's daily *pūjā*, when He is seen in all objects, and then He alone exists. Is there then any need to worship, if worshipper and the object of worship are One? There is no longer a necessity for worship. Still one may continue to do *pūjā* in the knowledge that the One who is beyond Manifestation is also immanent in His creation and thus also in *pūjā*.

As can be expected, Ānandamayī Mā deals at length with the role of a *guru* in relation to *sādhanā*. While Hinduism, on the whole, attaches great importance to the role of a *guru*, She considers it possible to engage in *sādhanā* without the bodily presence of a *guru*. In one way, She argues, everyone has a *guru*, since only One exists and the One manifesting through various people, objects, circumstances, teaches us, even though we may not be aware of it. Also, the quest for an outer *guru* will eventually lead to the discovery of the inner *guru*, one's true Self. She warns, however, that it is easy to mistake the prompting of one's mind for the inner *guru*. Only the one who is "free from anger, greed, delusion, pride, egotism" is attuned to the inner *guru*. Normally She advises devotees to look for an "outer" *guru*: "Go and sit under a tree...." The tree signifies a saint, a truly enlightened person who can lead one to God. "Saints may be compared to trees: they always point upwards and grant shade and shelter to all. They are free from likes and dislikes and whoever seeks refuge in them wholeheartedly, will find peace." She adds: "Just as water cleanses everything by its mere contact, even so the sight, touch, blessing, nay the very remembrance of a real *sādhu*, little by little, clears away all impure desires and longings." Finding a genuine *guru* is indeed a blessing. One must follow his advice unconditionally. While obeying the *guru* and treating him with reverence, one must not become attached to his personality. The true *guru* will naturally emphasize the fact that he is a mere vehicle of God and discourage personal ven-

Listening to the teachings of a *guru*

eration. It is the false *guru*—still in ego-consciousness—who permits the development of a personality cult. What if one unwittingly has found a false *guru*? Even this is only a seeming misfortune, for there will come a time when one awakens from one's error and then one will assuredly know how to discover a genuine *guru*. There is another aspect to be considered. More important than the *guru* is the devotee's own attitude, because in the ultimate sense, no one else can give us Self-realization. We have to find it. Thus it is conceivable that a sincere seeker, seeing God behind his *guru*, however imperfect that *guru* might be, will be able to go beyond the *guru* and reach God.

In one's *sādhanā* the *guru*'s help normally is particularly important for learning the art of concentration on God, i.e., meditation.

The restless mind, flitting from one aspect of this world of multiplicity to another, must be brought under control so that the many are eliminated and the One perceived. Numerous are the methods that *guru*s suggest to their disciples. Ānandamayī Mā tells the story of a *guru* who noticed that his disciple was making no progress in meditation. Thereupon the *guru* asked the disciple whether there was anyone or anything that interested him intensely. Without hesitation the disciple said that his main interest was his buffalo. "Then go to your meditation room and concentrate on the buffalo. Visualize him and do not let your mind wander from thinking about the buffalo." The following day the *guru* knocked at the door of the meditation room and asked the disciple to come out. There followed a period of silence. Then the disciple

replied in an exceedingly deep voice that it was impossible for him to leave his room, because his horns could not pass through the door. He obviously had achieved a high degree of concentration! The moral of the story is that deep concentration leads to identification, to merger. Actually, all human beings are potential *yogis* (one who practices *yoga* or has mastered it), able to concentrate on what interests them. For hours men can sit and play cards, watch movies or shows, or bend all their efforts to amassing money or passing examinations. All that is needed is a shift of emphasis from the worldly to God.

In agreement with the mystics of all ages in the East or in the West, Ānandamayī Mā points out that one of the greatest obstacles on the path back to God is our ego. "Always bear this in mind: Everything is in God's hands, and you are His tool to be used by Him as He pleases. Try to grasp the significance of 'all is His,' and you will immediately feel free from all burdens. What will be the result of your surrender to Him? None will seem alien, all will be your very own, your Self." The idea "I am apart, separate from everything else" must go. Man has to learn to empty himself completely of desire, pride, passion, and any awareness of "I am" or "I do." So long as we have not attained total emptiness, God, who is everything, cannot occupy us, cannot pour his infinite divine bliss into us. Ānandamayī Mā's view on emptiness is similar to the Zen concept of emptiness and the concept of the most intimate poverty (*eigentlichste Armut*) of Meister Eckhart who says: "…if God wants to act in the soul, He Himself must be the place in which He acts…."

Our discussion of *sādhanā* has been entirely concerned with spiritual matters so far. Does service to humanity have no part in one's *sādhanā*? This question obviously will occur to westerners among whom religion has at present almost become identified with social service. They are likely to ask whether Ānandamayī Mā is totally unconcerned about human welfare. Does She ignore the enormous physical suffering of the masses which is a most conspicuous and depressing element of Indian life? Melita Maschmann, the German novelist, in a way, addressed herself to this question. During her stay in Calcutta she met Mother Theresa, the Catholic nun who has dedicated her life to the founding of orphanages, medical centers, homes for the aged, in other words, has been engaged in social welfare work. Miss Maschmann mentioned to one of Ānandamayī Mā's disciples that it seemed to her that, in contradistinction to Ānandamayī Mā, the Catholic nun was truly living up to the commandment that one should love one's neighbor as oneself. The immediate reply of the disciple was that service to mankind was precisely what Ānandamayī Mā was doing all the time. Ānandamayī Mā would probably say that each one has to play a different role in God's cosmic drama. One role has been assigned to Mother Theresa, another to Ānandamayī Mā. Actually, She does stress the importance of helping others not only spiritually: "Widening your shriveled heart, make the interests of others your own and serve them as much as you can by sympathy, kindness, presents and so forth. So long as one enjoys the things of this world and has needs and wants, it is necessary to minister to the needs of one's fellowmen. Otherwise one cannot be called a human being. Whenever you have the opportunity, give to the poor, feed the hungry, nurse the sick.… Do service as a religious duty and you will come to know by direct perception that the person served, the one who serves, and the act of service are separate only in appearance."

While it is obvious that Ānandamayī Mā agrees that alleviating physical suffering, if carried out in a selfless spirit, contributes to one's spiritual advance, She herself, just as the Buddha, is concerned with getting at the root of all suffering, to eliminate it once and for all. Her diagnosis is that alienation from the One (one's true Self) is the basic cause of all suffering. Therefore by doing away with physical suffering one deals with the symptoms, not with the underlying cause of the disease. In fact, one-sided concentration on eliminating physical suffering may even prolong the disease. Here we must keep in mind that Ānandamayī Mā's whole teaching emphasizes the fact that all seemingly negative experiences ultimately have positive consequences. As has been stated earlier, suffering is really a means for ending suffering: "Just as fire burns away all dross and rubbish, so the

three-fold suffering purges man's heart from all impurity and results in a growing single-mindedness in his search after Truth. When he becomes deeply conscious of his weakness and tormented by the thought of his undesir- able impulses and distressing characteristics, when afflictions like poverty, bereavement, or humiliation make him feel his life is futile, then and then only does he develop real faith and religious fervor, and becomes anxious to surrender himself at the feet of the Supreme Being. Suffering should therefore be welcomed. Never does the soft moonlight appear more soothing than after the scorching heat of a summer day." The great promise is: "By sorrow does the Lord dispel sorrow and by adversity does He destroy adversity. When this is done He sends no more suffering—this must be borne in mind at all times."

Ānandamayī Mā's views on suffering and poverty are so diametrically opposed to the whole philosophy of modern western man that it would require revolutionary changes in his attitude for him to agree with Her. All our attempts to wipe out poverty and the doctors' frantic quest for eliminating physical pain are undertaken in the belief that perfection can be attained by physical means. They are based on a dualistic view of the universe which labels certain things as evil without acknowledging their redeeming potential. Above all, this applies to modern western man's aversion to suffering, which is regarded as an unmitigated evil. In contrast, Ānandamayī Mā holds up to us the attitude towards pain as exemplified in India's great epic, the *Rāmāyana*. There, Hanumān, the loyal devotee of Rāma (an *avatāra* of Viṣṇu), built a bridge to Lanka (Ceylon), in order to rescue Sītā, Rāma's consort, who had been abducted to Lanka by the demon King Rāvana. During the construction of the bridge, Hanumān accidentally hurt a squirrel. The squirrel thereupon complained to Rāma and demanded that in punishment Rāma step upon Hanumān. Rāma did so and told Hanumān not to commit such a deed again, if he did not want to suffer similar punishment. But Hanumān retorted: "I will very often commit such faults so that I may repeatedly feel the pressure of your feet."

Further to stress the purifying effect of suffering, Ānandamayī Mā tells the story of a pitcher which became a *pūjā* vessel. Originally it had been just an ordinary clump of earth on which people trampled and into which people dug with sharp spades. Later the earth was tak-

en to a potter who kneaded it and put it on a potter's wheel, turned it around, molded it and fired it to make it hard and solid. Only then was it fit to be used as a *pūjā* vessel and sacred Ganges water poured into it. Similarly human vessels have to be molded to become fit instruments for the divine spirit. "Be enduring as earth ... divine life will be awakened in you." By looking at suffering from a truly monistic point

of view, another dimension emerges: "Who is it that loves and who that suffers? He alone stages a play with Himself.... The individual suffers because he perceives duality.... Find the One everywhere and in everything and there will be an end to pain and suffering."

With Ānandamayī Mā's stress on finding the One as the cure-all, what is the role of renunciation? Is total renunciation required of those who are earnest about their *sādhanā*? Actually the mass of mankind are renunciants of a sort, for they renounce God, who is Supreme Bliss, for the sake of paltry temporary material pleasures. When that true Reality has been contacted, all cravings will drop off. "Worldly things seem tedious, quite foreign to oneself; worldly talk loses all its appeal, becomes devoid of interest and at a further stage even painful.... To the extent that one becomes estranged from the world of the senses one draws nearer to God. If man only knew that he is settling for synthetic pleasures while he could have real ever-lasting joy, the question of renunciation would not be a matter of struggle. As it is, only few are ready to pledge themselves formally to complete renunciation and become homeless wanderers (*saṁnyāsi*s). Ānandamayī Mā warns strongly against taking the vows of renunciation before one is truly prepared for this step. As long as one is inwardly plagued by cravings and prone to hatred, anger, and fear, withdrawing to the Himalayas is delusion. Mere outward renunciation will not do. Wearing the ochre robe of renunciation may help some to live up to their vows, but eventually one must reach a state where one is no longer in need of such a reminder. After all, even an ochre robe is part of delusion. It might also tempt one to spiritual pride. No hard and fast rules apply to any path. To illustrate this point She mentioned that She had met a man who had been a *saṁnyāsi*. After years of strenuous effort he had made no apparent spiritual progress and in desperation he had abandoned his life of renunciation. Shortly thereafter he attained enlightenment.

If one cannot vow oneself to total renunciation, one can use the life of a householder for spiritual advance. Untold opportunities arise in one's householder existence to practice *sādhanā*. One can serve God in the form of one's wife and children. One's home can become an *āśram* in which the whole family jointly worships. After a few children are born, husband and wife ought to live like brother and sister, forgoing sexual relations. In general, Ānandamayī Mā urges householders to pattern their lives upon those of the ancient *ṛṣi*s (seers, sages). Accordingly, when one approaches the age of fifty-five or sixty, one should withdraw from worldly activities. One has played one's part, fulfilled one's social duties. Wisdom demands that the remaining few years will be spent for God alone.

How different this is from modern western man's desperate attempts to prolong youth so that he can continue to indulge in sense pleasures, to avoid facing his Self! How much time and money he expends to hide signs of ageing! How great is his skill in devising new forms of entertainment to divert his attention from the thought of death! Ānandamayī Mā goes so far as to sanction withdrawing from family life at an earlier age, if one is consumed by the fire of renunciation. But by no means does She approve of withdrawal from marital obligations for those whose motive it is to evade family responsibilities. One's yearning for renunciation must be as intense as that of the Buddha who left his family to discover the cause of suffering. Significantly, the present Indian constitution has a provision granting divorce in cases where one marriage partner wishes to renounce the world. It is most unlikely that need for such legislation will occur in the United States.

By advocating a return to the life of the *ṛṣis*, Ānandamayī Mā clearly indicates Her preference for the value system of ancient India. In 1961, the then Governor of Maharashtra, Śrī Śrī Prakāśa, asked Her what cure She envisioned for the moral and spiritual decay of modern society. In reply She pleaded for a return to the ancient Vedic system whose foundation was *brahmacarya*, i.e., young men and women lived a celibate life and received spiritual training from their *guru* before embarking upon the householder path.[5] She considers the *brahmacarya* stage essential for a stable society. Only if young people are taught self-control, even-mindedness, unselfishness, and God-centeredness, would they be well-grounded in the art of living. Then *brahmacarya* would automatically lead to *brahmavidyā* (knowledge of *Brahman*, God). Traditional is also Ānandamayī Mā's attitude towards the selection of marriage partners. In view of the fact that young people are likely to base their choice of a marriage partner on physical attraction primarily, it is preferable that their parents make the choice. She takes it for granted that parents will have a more mature judgment than their offsprings and that they will give primary consideration to the welfare of their sons and daughters. This is indeed a noble ideal, but in practice many parents fail to live up to Her lofty standards. Bride and bridegroom should not see each other before the wedding. She compares such an act to offering for *pūjā* a fruit that has been pecked at by a bird.

With Her strong emphasis on the sacredness of marital ties, it is not surprising that Ānandamayī Mā counsels: "There is only one marriage." Consequently She never advises a second marriage even for widows. It should be pointed out, however, that She in no way discriminates against those who come to Her who have already been married twice or even three times.

Her attitude towards the role of women is both traditional and modern. She does emphasize woman's duty to be loyal and obedient to Her husband. At the same time She envisages a revolutionary change in the status of women: "It marks the spirit of the present time that women will take their place at the helm of society and men ply the oars." The spiritual training of women must not in any way be inferior to that of men. "Then you will see how the lives of both men and women will be ennobled and raised to a higher level … a renaissance of Hindu society will follow." Does Ānandamayī Mā possibly conceive Her own role as a spiritual leader characteristic of the new age? She has in fact taken several concrete steps to demonstrate the changed status of women. Not only did She perform the sacred thread ceremony—a monopoly of men for many hundred years—upon Herself, but in 1940 also arranged for it to be performed upon three of Her women devotees.[6] Consequently all three of them recite regularly

---

[5] Only in the early Vedic Age (1500-800 B.C.) do women seem to have received a formal religious education.

[6] Four other *brahmacāriṇī*s have been given sacred threads in recent years.

the *gāyatrī mantra*,[7] normally reserved for men. In 1965 a *Nārāyana Śilā* (blackish stone, a symbol of Lord Nārāyana) was brought to Ānandamayī Mā. The bliss-permeated Mother thereupon instructed a woman renunciant, Brahmacārinī Udās, to perform regular *pūjā* of the *Nārāyana Śilā*. Again, this was contrary to

[7] Sacred *mantra* of the *Rig Veda*, a hymn to the sun, recited daily by Hindus of the three upper castes, after they have been invested with the sacred thread.

tradition. When, upon the death of Her husband, Her mother, Didimā, decided to take the vow of renunciation, a distinguished *guru*, Swāmī Mangal Giri, was approached. At first he declined to accept Didimā as a complete renunciant. Obviously through the intercession of Ānandamayī Mā he relented. Didimā became Swāmī Muktānanda Giri. This too was most uncommon, for the title *swāmī* (master) is rarely conferred upon a woman.

It is necessary not to misconstrue Ānandamayī Mā's innovative gestures. In no way can they be seen as woman's liberationist moves in the western sense. The emphasis is on spiritual equality. Above all, the goal is liberation from sense enslavement and egocentricity. This is contrary to the contemporary western movement which chiefly claims the right for women to indulge in sense and pursue egotistic goals on par with men.

Ānandamayī Mā also holds traditional views towards food. She considers it important to eat sattvic (pure) foods, i.e. no meat, fish, eggs, garlic, or onions. She does, however, broaden the concept of food to mean anything taken in by one's mind or senses. Man, therefore, should abstain from impure thoughts and feelings, such as lust, greed, hatred, envy, and anger. Naturally, pure thoughts take precedence over pure food. And yet repeatedly Ānandamayī Mā makes it clear that it is unwise to belittle ritual, to think that one may easily do away with the externals. There is a subtle interrelationship between internal and external worship. It is on those grounds that She upholds traditional religious ceremonies including *yajñas* (fire sacrifices). From 1947 to 1950 a giant fire sacrifice was performed at Her *āśram* in Vārāṇasi, with the participation of holy men from all over India.

Her respect for tradition even extends to the institution of caste which, for a westerner, is most difficult to understand. At a time when many intellectuals in India condemn the caste system and the Indian constitution has, in theory at least, outlawed it, caste restrictions are

enforced in the *āśram*s of Ānandamayī Mā. The bliss-permeated Mother Herself is beyond caste. Just as did India's greatest philosopher, Śaṅkarācārya, She can say: "No birth, no death, no caste have I." All human beings are equal in Her eyes. But the majority of those who surround Her are strictly orthodox and concerned about contamination. Foreigners who seek *darśana* from Ānandamayī Mā discover that they are treated as casteless. They must eat and sleep separately and avoid coming close to the kitchen, for their very presence in the kitchen would contaminate the food. These rules apply even to Brahmacāriṇī Ātmānanda. Melita Maschmann in particular was disturbed about this seemingly inconsistent attitude of Ānandamayī Mā. After all, if only One exists, why stress caste distinctions? In a talk with Ānandamayī Mā she aired

Ānandamayī Mā at the Vārāṇasi *āśram*

View of the Vārāṇasi *āśram* from the Ganges

her feelings. The Mother then explained that during Her *sādhanā* She had behaved in a most unconventional manner and therefore alienated many orthodox Hindus. Once She had consulted a *mahātmā* who had advised Her to abide by Hindu traditions, otherwise She would keep away the orthodox element of the population. While She Herself continued to treat everyone alike irrespective of caste background, She decided not to interfere with the enforcement of caste rules. She was fully aware of the fact that foreigners incurred some hardships thereby, but since there were only a handful of foreigners involved, She did not deem it right to make it impossible for orthodox Hindus to enjoy Her presence. The majority of Her followers were still living on a level of consciousness where abidance by caste restrictions was important for

them. At the right time they would transcend caste feeling, but one could not artificially accelerate this development. She seems convinced that the time for abolishing the caste system has not arrived. Such an attitude must be totally incomprehensible to western activists engaged in social crusades.

Western Faustian man, whose dynamism is fed by the notion of progress, will not be enamored by Ānandamayī Mā's view of progress. Once during a trip to Baidyanāth Dhām in 1938, Ānandamayī Mā was shown newly built houses which starkly contrasted with some old dilapidated buildings in the background. But Ānandamayī Mā was not impressed. She pointed out to Didi that there had been a time when the old houses had been brand new. Rise and decay are the eternal *leitmotif* in the realm of

View of the Ganges outside the Annapurna temple at the Vārāṇasi *āśram*

Left: Akhandanānda Smriti Mandir (memorial temple), dedicated to Swami Akhandanāndajī (Didi's father) at the Vārāṇasi *āśram*
Right: Annapurna temple at the Vārāṇasi *āśram*

matter. Is it then futile to try to make improvements? She sees nothing wrong in technical advance, provided it is used for spiritual ends. After all, She Herself now uses trains and motor cars to travel to various places. When Her beloved devotee Dr. Gopīnāth Kavirāj was very ill, She saw to it that he was placed in a modern hospital with the most up-to-date equipment. It is technical progress for mere progress' sake that She rejects. Basing one's philosophy on material progress alone is like building a house on a foundation of sand. The ultimate criterion for deciding any problem must be: "Will this action lead me towards God-realization or not?" This is the kind of pragmatism which is wholly alien to materialists. Ānandamayī Mā could ask the hardheaded western realists whether technological progress had done away with greed, hatred, fear. Has it supplied man with peace and bliss? In view of the fact that more and more westerners begin to have second thoughts about technological progress, the views of Ānandamayī Mā may have more relevance for us than we may at first admit. To those who seek perfection She suggests self-perfection; to those in search of a revolution, self-revolution; and to those suffering from alienation she offers oneness with the very source of their being. "Only actions that kindle man's divine nature are worthy of the name of action…. Man's calling is to aspire to the realization of Truth, to tread the excellent path that leads to immortality."

At the Congress of Indian Philosophy held in Dacca in 1929 someone asked Ānandamayī Mā: "If the human character and everybody becomes unselfish, will the world then become perfect?" Her answer was: "But such it is already." She sees a harmony that escapes us, who are still enmeshed in delusion, mesmerized by the world's apparent duality. She is exuding bliss because She is in constant contact with that One whom the Hindus define as *Sat-Cit-Ānanda* (Being-Consciousness-Bliss). But that bliss of Hers is of little use to us unless we too experience it. Therefore She urges us: "Become drinkers of nectar, all of you—drinkers of the wine of immortality. Tread the path of immortality, where no death exists and no disease."

आनन्दमयीघाट

Ānandamayī Mā *āśram* at Vārāṇasi

Ānandamayī Mā's room at the Vārāṇasi *āśram*

Shrine of Kṛṣṇa Gopal at the Vārāṇasi *āśram*

CHAPTER III

Selected Discourses

The following are selections from Śrī Ānandamayī Mā's replies to oral questions, recorded at meetings of large and small groups. The recorder of the discussions, Brahmacāri Kamal Bhattacharjee, well-known as "Kamalda" to all devotees and visitors of Ānandamayī Mā, first met Mātājī in Dacca in 1926, and kept in touch with her ever since. In 1942 he joined the Vārāṇasi *āśram* and became one of its most devoted and prominent workers. Gifted with a keen intelligence and a great thirst for real knowledge, he conceived the intense desire to record Mātājī's exact words, since he was convinced that they emerged spontaneously from depths to which ordinary human beings have no access. Notwithstanding his numerous duties as the Joint Secretary of the Shree Shree Anandamayee Sangha and the manager of the Vārāṇasi *āśram*, etc., as soon as he got to know that Mātājī was replying to questions, he would at once leave the work in hand, and hasten to the spot where the discussion took place. In his eagerness to preserve Mātājī's utterances in their original purity and with the greatest possible precision, he soon developed a technique of his own. In the stillness of night he used to make fair copies of his records, pondering over the profound significance of what he had heard and written down. Often the dawn would remind him that he had spent the best part of the night in this delightful meditation. If, for some reason, he was prevented from recording a part of the conversation, he felt it as an acute personal loss. But on many such occasions, he would later, to his great delight, hear Mātājī explain the same point to someone else, thereby elucidating the part of the conversation he had missed.

Mātājī speaks of that which is beyond the experience of the ordinary individual and can, at best, be only hinted at by words. It is therefore not surprising that her language should not conform to either literary or colloquial Bengali. She has given new meanings to many familiar expressions and sometimes coined new words with an etymology of her own. Her way of expression is as original as it is relevant, and is intensely alive and plastic, often condensed and pithy, with every unnecessary word left out. In certain cases, when stating very profound truths, her language becomes cryptic. The dissimilarity of the Bengali idiom to that of English is a well-known fact. No adequate words exist in English for many Bengali terms. In some cases two or three Bengali words have had to be rendered by an entire clause or sentence. No pains have been spared to translate as precisely as possible every one of the utterances, as recorded. At the same time, it has been the ambition of the translator as much as possible to preserve, together with the exact meaning of the words, their rhythm and beauty, the inspiration they carry, and the matchless, intangible quality that pervades Mātājī's every expression—her words, her songs, her smile, and her gestures.

———

Concerning the value of religious and philosophical discourses, Mātājī said:

By listening repeatedly to discussions and discourses on topics of this kind, the path to first-hand knowledge of what has been heard gradually opens out. You know, it is as when water uninterruptedly dripping on a stone finally makes a hole in it, and then a flood may suddenly surge through, which will bring enlightenment.

Be it the perusal of Sacred Texts, listening to religious discourses, engaging in *kīrtana*—God must be the alpha and omega of whatever is done. When reading, read about Him, when talking, talk of Him, and when singing, sing His praises. These three practices are intrinsically the same; but because people respond differently, the same is expressed in three different ways to suit each person's temperament and capacity for assimilation. Essentially there is only He and He alone, although everyone has his own individual path that leads to Him. What is the right path for each depends on his personal predilection, based on the specific character of his inner qualifications.

Take for instance the study of *Vedānta*. Some seekers become completely drowned in it. Just as others may so lose themselves in *kīrtana* as to fall into a trance, a student of *Vedānta* may become wholly absorbed in his texts, even more so than the one who gets carried away by *kīrtana*. According to one's specific line of approach, one will be able to achieve full concentration through the study of a particular Scripture, or by some other means.

First comes listening, then reflection, and last of all the translation into action of what has been heard and pondered over. This is why one has first of all to listen, so that later on each may be able to select *Vedānta* or *kīrtana* or whatever else be in his own line.

Have you never come across people making light of *kīrtana*, saying: "What is there to be gained by it?" Nevertheless, after listening to it for some length of time, they actually develop a liking for it. Therefore one must listen before one can reflect, and then later, what has been heard and reflected upon will take shape in action suited to the person concerned. To listen to discourses on God or Truth is certainly beneficial, provided one does not allow oneself to be moved by a spirit of fault-finding or disparagement, should there be differences of outlook to one's own. To find fault with others creates obstacles for everyone all around: for him who criticizes, for him who is blamed, as well as for those who listen to the criticism. Whereas, what is said in a spirit of appreciation is fruitful to everybody. For only where there is no question of regarding anything as inferior or blameworthy (*asat*) can one call it *satsaṅga*.[1]

Who is known as a *vaiṣṇava*? One who sees Viṣṇu everywhere. And as a *śākta*? One who beholds the Great Mother and nothing save Her. In truth, all the various ways of thought spring from one common source—who then is to be blamed, who to be reviled or suppressed? All are equal in essence.

Thou art Mother, Thou art Father,
Thou art Friend and Thou art Master,
Truly, Thou art all in all.
Every name is Thy Name,
Every quality Thy Quality,
Every form Thy Form indeed.

Yet He is also where no forms exist, as pure unmanifested Being—all depends on one's avenue of approach.

For this reason, no matter what path anyone may choose it is THAT. *Vedānta* actually means the end of difference and non-difference.[2] While engaging in *sādhanā* one must concentrate in a single direction; but after it has been completed, what comes then? The cessation of difference, distinction, and disagreement. Differences do indeed exist on the path, but how can there be a difference of goal?

---

1 A play upon words: *Sat* means true Being, the Good; *satsaṅga* the company of the good, and also a religious gathering. *Asat*, the opposite of *sat*, means non-being, wrong, evil. Therefore to find fault (*asat*) in a religious meeting (*satsaṅga*) is a contradiction in terms.

2 *Vedānta*: end or culmination of Vedic wisdom. Mātājī here plays upon words: *Veda*, and *bheda* (difference). In Bengali the letters B and V sound alike. "*Anta*" means "end."

A member of a well-known Indian family, who had distinguished herself by devoting her life to social service, came for Mātājī's *darśana* and asked:

Does the capacity to meditate come by practice in this life, or is it an aptitude acquired in former births?

Mātājī: It may be the result of either of the two, or of both combined. Meditation should be practiced every day of one's life. Look, what is there in this world? Absolutely nothing that is lasting; therefore direct your longing towards the Eternal. Pray that the work done through you, His instrument, may be pure. In every action remember Him. The purer your thinking, the finer will be your work. In this world you get a thing, and by tomorrow it may be gone. This is why your life should be spent in a spirit of service; feel that the Lord is accepting services from you in whatever you do. If you desire peace you must cherish the thought of Him.

Question: *When will there be peace on earth?*

Mātājī: Well, you know what the present state of affairs is; things are happening as they are destined to be.

Question: *When will this state of unrest come to an end?*

Mātājī: *Jagat* (world) means ceaseless movement, and obviously there can be no rest in movement. How could there be peace in perpetual coming and going? Peace reigns where no coming exists and no going, no melting and no burning. Reverse your course, advance towards Him—then there will be hope of peace.

By your *japa* and meditation those who are close to you will also benefit through the helpful influence of your presence. In order to develop a taste for meditation you have to make a deliberate and sustained effort, just as children have to be made to sit and study, be it by persuasion or coercion. By taking medicine or having injections a patient may get well; even if you do not feel inclined to meditate, conquer your reluctance and make an attempt. The habit of countless lives is pulling you in the opposite direction and making it difficult for you—persevere in spite of it! By your tenacity you will gain strength and be molded; that is to say, you will develop the capability to do *sādhanā*. Make up your mind that however arduous the task, it will have to be accomplished. Recognition and fame last for a short time only, they do not accompany you when you leave this world. If your thought does not naturally turn towards the Eternal, fix it there by an effort of will. Some severe blow of fate will drive you towards God. This will be but an expression of His mercy; however painful, it is by such blows that one learns one's lesson.

A Government Official and his wife had come for Mātājī's *darśana*. They were meeting her for the first time. To a question of theirs, Mātājī replied:

If you say you have no faith, you should try to establish yourself in the conviction that you have no faith. Where "no" is, "yes" is potentially there as well. Who can claim to be beyond negation and affirmation? To have faith is imperative. The natural impulse to have faith in something, which is deep-rooted in man, develops into faith in God. This is why human birth is such a great boon. It cannot be said that no one has faith. Everyone surely believes in something or other.

There are two kinds of pilgrims on life's journey: the one, like a tourist, is keen on sightseeing, wandering from place to place, flitting from one experience to another for the fun of it. The other treads the path that is consistent with man's true being and leads to his real home, to Self-knowledge. Sorrow will of a certainty be encountered on the journey undertaken for the sake of sight-seeing and enjoyment. So long as one's real home has not been found, suffering is inevitable. The sense of separateness is the root-cause of misery, because it is founded on error, on the conception of duality.

A man's belief is greatly influenced by his environment; therefore he should choose the company of the holy and wise. Belief means to believe in one's Self, disbelief to mistake the non-Self for one's Self.

There are instances of Self-realization occurring by the grace of God, whereas at other times it can be seen that He awakens in some a feverish yearning after Truth. In the first case attainment comes spontaneously, in the second it is brought about by trials. But all is wrought solely by His mercy.

An eternal relationship exists between God and man. But in His play it is sometimes there and sometimes severed, or rather appears to be severed; it is not really so, for the relationship is eternal. Again, seen from another side, there is no such thing as relationship. Someone who came to meet this body, said: "I am a newcomer to you." He got the reply: "Ever new and ever old indeed!"

The light of the world comes and goes, it is unstable. The light that is eternal can never be extinguished. By this light you behold the outer light and everything in the universe; it is only because It shines ever within you that you can perceive the outer light. Whatever appears to you in the universe is due solely to that great light within you, and only because the supreme knowledge of the essence of things lies hidden in the depths of your being is it possible for you to acquire knowledge of any kind.

Inquirer: *It is all in God's hands.*

Mātājī: Everything is in God's hands, and you are His tool to be used by Him as He pleases. Try to grasp the significance of "all is His," and you will immediately feel free from all burdens. What will be the result of your surrender to Him? None will seem alien, all will be your very own, your Self.

Either melt by devotion the sense of separateness, or burn it by knowledge—for what is it that melts or burns? Only that which by its nature can be melted or burnt; namely the idea that something other than your Self exists. What will happen then? You come to know your Self.

By virtue of the *guru's* power everything becomes possible; therefore seek a *guru*. Mean-while, since all names are His Name, all forms His Form, select one of them and keep it with you as your constant companion. At the same time He is also nameless and formless; for the Supreme it is possible to be everything and yet nothing. So long as you have not found a *guru*, adhere to the name or form of Him that appeals to you most, and ceaselessly pray that He may reveal Himself to you as the *Sadguru*.[3] In very truth the *guru* dwells within, and unless you discover the inner *guru*, nothing can be achieved. If you feel no desire to turn to God, bind yourself by a daily routine of *sādhanā*, as

[3] The perfect *guru* who shows the way to the knowledge of Reality.

school children do, whose duty it is to follow a fixed time-table.

When prayer does not spontaneously flow from your heart, ask yourself: "Why do I find pleasure in the fleeting things of this world?" If you crave for some outer thing or feel specially attracted to a person, you should pause and say to yourself: "Look out, you are being fascinated by the glamour of this!" Is there a place where God is not? Family life, which is the *āśrama* (life stage) of the householder, can also take you in His direction, provided it is accepted as an *āśrama*. Lived in this spirit, it helps man to progress towards Self-realization. Nevertheless, if you hanker after anything such as name, fame, or position, God will bestow it on you, but you will not feel satisfied. The kingdom of God is a whole, and unless you are admitted to the whole of it you cannot remain content. He grants you just a little, only to keep your discontent alive, for without discontent there can be no progress. You, a scion of the Immortal, can never become reconciled to the realm of death, neither does God allow you to remain in it. He Himself kindles the sense of want in you by granting you a small thing, only to whet your appetite for a greater one. This is His method by which He urges you on. The traveler on this path finds it difficult and feels troubled, but one who has eyes to see can clearly perceive that the pilgrim is advancing. The distress that is experienced burns to ashes all pleasure derived from worldly things. This is what is called *tapasyā*.[4] What obstructs one on the spiritual path bears within itself seeds of future suffering. Yet the heartache, the anguish over the effects of these obstructions, are the beginning of an awakening to consciousness.

———

A young girl was talking to Mātājī. She said:

[4] Hardships undergone with the definite object of attaining to the spiritual.

When I sit down to meditate I do not intend to contemplate any form, but how is it possible to meditate on the formless? I have noticed that at times, when I try to meditate, images of deities come floating before my mind.

Mātājī: Whatever image arises in your mind, that you should contemplate; just observe in what shape God will manifest Himself to you. The same form does not suit every person. For some Rāma may be most helpful, for some Śiva, for others Pārvatī, and again for others the formless. He certainly is formless; but at the same time, watch in what particular form He may appear to you in order to show you the way. Consequently, whichever of His forms comes into your mind, that you should contemplate in all its minute details.

Proceed as follows: When sitting down to meditate, first of all contemplate the form of a deity; then, imagining Him to be enthroned on His seat, bow down before Him and do *japa*. When you have concluded the *japa* bow down once more and, having enshrined Him in your heart, leave your seat. This, in short, may be your practice if you are not able to meditate on the *Brahman*.

Be ever convinced that at all times and without exception He will do and is doing what is best for you. Reflect thus: In order to aid me, He has revealed Himself to me in this particular guise. He is with form as well as without; the entire universe is within Him and pervaded by Him. This is why it is said: "The *Sadguru* is the World-teacher and the World-teacher the *Sadguru*."

———

In reply to a question concerning the way of reaching *samādhi*, Mātājī said:

Mātājī: It is for the *guru* to point out the method; he will show you the way to understanding and instruct you in your *sādhanā*. It is for you to keep on practicing it faithfully. But the fruit comes spontaneously in the form of

Self-revelation. The power to make you grasp the Ungraspable duly manifests itself through the *guru*. Where the question "How am I to proceed?" arises, fulfillment has obviously not yet been reached. Therefore, never relax your efforts until there is enlightenment. Let no gaps interrupt your attempt, for a gap will produce an eddy, whereas your striving must be continuous like the flowing of oil, it must be sustained, constant, an unbroken stream.

That you have no control over the body's need of food and sleep does not matter; your aim should be not to allow any interval in the performance of your *sādhanā*. Do you not see that whatever you require in the way of food and sleep, each at its own appointed hour, is without exception an ever-recurring need? In exactly the same manner must you aspire at uninterruptedness where the search after Truth is concerned. Once the mind, in the course of its movement, has felt the touch of the Indivisible—if only you can grasp that moment!—in that supreme moment all moments are contained, and when you have captured it, all moments will be yours.

Take, for example, the moments of confluence at dawn, midday, and dusk, in which the power inherent in the contact-point, where coming and going meet, becomes revealed. What you call "electric discharge" is nothing but the union of two opposites—thus does the Supreme Being flash forth at the moment of conjunction. Actually IT is present at every single moment, but you miss it all the time. Yet this is what you have to seize; it can be done at the point of juncture where the opposites fuse into one. Nobody is able to predict when for any particular individual this fateful moment will reveal itself; therefore keep on striving ceaselessly.

Which exactly is that great moment depends for each one upon his particular line of approach. This is why, for some disciples, the *guru* fixes special times for *sādhanā*, such as dawn, dusk, midday, and midnight; these are the four periods usually prescribed. It is the duty of the disciple to carry out conscientiously the *guru's* orders, which vary according to the temperament and predisposition of the aspirant. The same method does not suit everyone. What is important for you is the moment at which you

will enter the current that is the movement of your true being, the going forth, in other words, the great pilgrimage.

Within the twenty-four hours of the day, some time must be definitely dedicated to God. Resolve, if possible, to engage regularly in *japa* of a particular name or *mantra* while sitting in a special posture, and gradually add to the time or the number of repetitions. Fix the rate and the interval at which you will increase, say fortnightly or weekly. In this way try to bind yourself to the quest of God; wherever you may be, take refuge in Him, let Him be your goal. When by virtue of this endeavor you become deeply immersed in that current and devote ever more time to it, you will be transformed and your appetite for sense enjoyment will grow feeble; thus you will reap the fruit of your accumulated efforts. You may also come to feel that the body is liable to depart at any time, that death may arrive at any moment.

Who can tell at what moment the flame of illumination will blaze forth? For this reason, continue your efforts steadily without flagging. Gradually you will get more and more deeply absorbed in Him—He and He alone will preoccupy your thoughts and feelings. For the mind ever seeks that which gives it proper sustenance, and this cannot be provided by anything save the Supreme Being Himself. Then you will be carried away by the current that leads to your Self. You will discover that the more you delight in the inner life, the less you feel drawn to external things. In consequence the mind becomes so well nourished with the right kind of food, that at any moment the realization of its identity with the Self may occur.

There are instances when one loses consciousness while sitting in meditation. Some people have found themselves swooning away, as it were, intoxicated with joy, remaining in this condition for quite a long time. On emerging they claim to have experienced some sort of divine bliss. But this is certainly not realization. A stage does exist in meditation where intense joy is felt, where one is as if submerged in it. But what is it that gets submerged? The mind of course. At a certain level and under certain circumstances this experience may prove an obstacle. If repeated time and again, one may stagnate at its particular level and thereby be prevented from getting a taste of the Essence.

In the event of an experience of anything pertaining to ultimate Reality or to the Self, one does not say: "Where have I been? I did not know anything for the time being." There can be no such thing as "not knowing." One must be fully conscious, wide awake. To fall into a stupor or into yogic sleep will not take one anywhere.

After genuine contemplation (*dhyāna*) worldly pleasures become unalluring, dull, entirely savorless. What does *vairāgya* (detachment) signify? When every single object of the world kindles, as it were, the fire of renunciation, so as to make one recoil as from a shock, then there is inward and outward awakening. This, however, does not mean that *vairāgya* implies aversion or contempt for anything of the world—it simply is unacceptable, the body refuses it. Neither dislike nor anger will arise. When *vairāgya* becomes a living inspiration, one begins to discriminate as to the true nature of the world, until finally, with the glowing certainty of direct perception, the knowledge of its illusoriness arises. Each and everything belonging to the world seems to burn; one cannot touch it. This also is a state that may ensue at a particular time.

At present, what you enjoy does not impress you as being short-lived, rather does it appear to make you happy. But to the extent that the spirit of detachment is roused, the relish of such pleasures will die down, for are they not fleeting? In other words, death will die. Now that you are advancing towards that which is beyond time, the semblance of happiness brought about by mundane things is being consumed. As a result, the question "What actually is this world?" will arise. So long as the world seems enjoy-

able to you, such a query does not present itself. Since you are progressing towards that which transcends time, all that belongs to time will begin to appear to you in its true light.

Question: *At times we feel that sense objects really exist, at other times that they are merely ideas. Why does one and the same thing appear so different on different occasions?*

Mātājī: Because you are in the grip of time. You have not yet reached the state where everything is perceived as the Self alone,[5] have you? Herein lies the solution of the whole problem. To feel as you do is good, since your feeling is related to the supreme quest; for nothing is ever wasted. What you have realized even for a second will, at some time or other, bear fruit. Thus, the knowledge of the real character of each element (*tattva*)[6] and the knowledge what water, air, the sky, etc. are, and hence what creation is, will flash into your consciousness one by one—just like buds bursting open. Flowers and fruit come into existence only because they are potentially contained in the tree. Therefore you should aim at realizing the one supreme element (*tattva*) that will throw light on all elements.

You asked about sense objects: an object of sense is that which contains poison,[7] is full of harm, and drags man towards death. But freedom from the world of sense objects—where no trace of poison remains—means immortality.

Inquirer: *One is pulled in two directions, towards God as well as towards sense enjoyment—this causes anguish.*

Mātājī: You have a desire to give up, but you cannot let go; such is your problem. Let that desire awaken in your heart—its stirring signifies that the time is coming when you will be able to give up.

[5] A play upon words: *samaya* and *svamayī* sound alike. *Samaya*, time; *svamayī*, "permeated by Self."

[6] Literally "that-ness" or "essence." The *tattva*s are the primary elements or categories of universal manifestation.

[7] A play on words: *Viṣaya* means "sense object," *viṣ* "poison," *hai* "is."

You obtain a coveted object, but still you are dissatisfied; and if you fail to get it, you are also disappointed. The disillusionment you experience at the fulfillment of your wish is wholesome; but the torment of the unfulfilled hankering after the things you could not secure,

drives you towards that which is of death, towards misery.

Question: *And the anguish of not having found, the anguish of the absence of God? I have no wish for sense pleasures, but they come to me. I am compelled to experience them.*

Mātājī: Ah, but the anguish of not having found God is salutary. What you have eaten will leave a taste in your mouth. You wear ornaments because you wish to, and so you have to bear their weight. Yet this weight is fated to fall off, for it is something that cannot last, can it?

In reply to a question concerning visions and ecstasies, Mātājī said:

To lose control over oneself is not desirable. In the search after Truth one must not allow oneself to be overpowered by anything, but should watch carefully whatever phenomena may supervene, keeping fully conscious, wide awake, in fact retaining complete mastery over oneself. Loss of consciousness and of self-control are never right. There was a young man—into what supernormal states he used to pass, how many kinds of visions he had! He would, for example, do *pranām*[8] and remain in that posture for hours together, without raising his head, tears streaming down his cheeks. He declared that he saw and heard Śrī Kṛṣṇa teaching Arjuna, as described in the *Gītā*, and that he used to have many other visions and locutions of the kind. This body told him that, if a *sādhikā* could not maintain firm control over his mind, he would be liable to see and hear many things, both illusory and genuine, all mixed up. He might even be subjected to the influence of some "spirit" or power. Such occurrences, far from creating pure divine aspiration, would rather hinder than help. Moreover, to see someone in a vision or to hear him address you,

may well become a source of self-satisfaction or egotistic enjoyment.

The Lord Buddha is Himself the essence of enlightenment. All partial manifestations of wisdom that come in the course of *sādhanā* culminate in supreme enlightenment. In a similar way, supreme knowledge or supreme love may be attained. As there is a state of supreme Self-knowledge, likewise is there a state of perfection at the zenith of the path of love. There one finds the nectar of perfect love identical with supreme knowledge. In this state there is no room for emotional excitement; indeed, that would make it impossible for supreme love to shine forth. Be mindful of one thing: if, when following a particular line of approach, one does not attain to that which is the consummation of all *sādhanā*, namely the final goal, it means that one has not really entered that line. At the supreme summit of love, exuberance, excessive emotion, and the like cannot possibly occur. Emotional excitement and supreme love are in no wise to be compared; they are totally different from one another.

While absorbed in meditation, whether one is conscious of the body or not, whether there be a sense of identification with the physical or not—under all circumstances, it is imperative to remain wide awake; unconsciousness must be strictly avoided. Some genuine perceptivity must be retained, whether one contemplates the Self as such, or any particular form. What is the outcome of such meditation? It opens up one's being to the light, to that which is eternal. Suppose the body had been suffering from some pain or stiffness—lo and behold, after meditation it feels perfectly hale and hearty, with not a trace of fatigue or debility. It is as if a short period of time had elapsed in between, as if there had never been a question of any discomfort. This would be a good sign. But if tempted at the first touch of bliss to allow oneself to be drowned in it, and later to declare: "Where I was, I cannot say, I do not know,"—this is not desirable. As one becomes capable of real medi-

---

[8] Obeisance; an act of surrender, indicating the sense of one's own smallness in the presence of the superior.

tation, and to the extent that one contacts Reality, one discovers the ineffable joy that lies hidden even in all outer objects.

If on the other hand one loses oneself as it were, lapsing into a kind of stupor while engaged in meditation, and afterwards claims to have been steeped in intense bliss, this sort of bliss is a hindrance. If the life-force seems to have been in abeyance—just as one has a sense of great happiness after sound sleep—it indicates stagnation. It is a sign of attachment, and this attachment stands in the way of true meditation, since one will be apt to revert to this state again and again; although from the standpoint of the world, which is altogether different, it would seem a source of profound inward joy and therefore certainly an indication of spiritual progress. To be held up at any stage is an obstacle to further progress—it simply means one has stopped advancing.

While engaging in meditation, one should think of oneself as a purely spiritual being, as Self-luminous, poised in the bliss of the Self, and in accordance with the *guru*'s instructions, try to concentrate on one's Iṣṭa.[9] The young man previously mentioned (the one who used to have visions) was intelligent, and therefore able to understand this sort of reasoning. As a result, the spectacular experiences ceased, and he now attends to his meditation and other spiritual exercises in a very quiet, unobtrusive manner.

Later, when the conversation reverted to meditation (*dhyāna*) and the subject of bodily postures (*āsana*s), Mātājī said:

Look, if you spend hour after hour sitting in a certain posture, if you become absorbed while in that pose and are unable to meditate in any other, it shows that you are deriving enjoyment from the posture; this also constitutes an obstacle. When one first starts practicing *japa* and meditation, it is of course right to try and continue in the same position for as long as possible. But as one approaches perfection

in these practices, the question as to how long one has remained in one posture does not arise; at any time and in any position—lying, sitting, standing, or leaning over to one side, as the case may be—one can no longer be deterred by anything from the contemplation of one's Ideal or the Beloved.

The first sign of progress comes when one feels ill at ease in anything but a meditative pose. Nothing external interests one; the only thing that seems attractive is to be seated in one's favorite posture as long as possible and to contemplate the supreme object of one's worship, plunged in a deep inner joy. This marks the beginning of single-mindedness, and hence is a step in the right direction. If one stays in that position, as long as the inclination lasts—confident that the Beloved can never do one harm—and if one is able to remain fixed in it, then the posture becomes of overwhelming importance. This only shows that one is nearing perfection in the practice of *āsana*. Standing, sitting, walking—in fact, any gesture taken up by the body is called an *āsana*. It corresponds to the rhythm and the vibration of body and mind at any particular moment. Some aspirants can meditate only if seated in the pose indicated by the *guru* or formulated in the *Śāstra*s, and not otherwise. This is the way to proficiency in meditation. On the other hand, someone may begin his practice while sitting in any ordinary position; nevertheless, as soon as the state of *japa* or *dhyāna* has been reached, the body will spontaneously take up the most appropriate position, after the manner that a hiccup happens involuntarily. As one's meditation grows more and more intense, the postures will of themselves correspondingly gain in perfection.

In true meditation Reality is contacted, and just as the touch of fire leaves an impression, this contact also leaves its mark. What happens as a result? Impediments fall away—they are either consumed by *vairāgya*, or melted by devotion to the Divine. Worldly things seem dull and insipid, quite foreign to oneself: worldly

---

[9] Literally "Beloved." The chosen deity one worships.

talk loses all its appeal, becomes devoid of interest, and at a further stage even painful. When a person's earthly possessions are lost or damaged, the victim feels disturbed, which gives evidence of the stranglehold that sense objects exercise over men's minds. This is what is called *granthi*—the knots constituting the I-ness. By meditation, *japa*, and other spiritual practices, which vary according to each one's individual line of approach, these knots become loosened, discrimination is developed, and one comes to discern the true nature of the world of sense

perception. In the beginning one was enmeshed in it, struggling helplessly in its net. As one becomes disentangled from it, and gradually passes through various stages of opening oneself more and more to the light, one comes to see that everything is contained in everything, that there is only one Self, the Lord of all, or that all are but the servants of the one Master. The form this realization takes depends upon one's orientation. One knows by direct perception that, as one exists, so everyone else exists; then again, that there is the One and nothing but the One, that nothing comes and goes, yet also does come and go—there is no way of expressing all this in words. To the extent that one becomes estranged from the world of the senses, one draws nearer to God.

———

Question: *Does the body survive when the ego-mind has been dissolved?*

Mātājī: At times the question is asked: "How does the World-teacher give instruction? From the state of *ajñāna*?" If this were so, the mind would not have been dissolved, the three-fold differentiation of the knower, the knowing, and the known, could not have been merged. So what would He be able to give you? Where could He lead you? But there is a stage where this question does not arise. Is it the body that is the obstacle to supreme knowledge? Is there even a question of whether the body exists or not? At a certain level this question is simply not there. On the plane where this question arises, one is not in the state of pure Being, and one thinks this question can be raised and also replied to. But the answer lies where there is no such thing as questioning and answering— where there are no "others," no division. This is one aspect of the matter.

Some say a last vestige of the mind remains. At a certain level this is so; however, there is a stage beyond, where the question of whether a trace of the mind remains or not, does not exist. If everything can be burnt up, cannot this last vestige be consumed too? There is no question of either "yes" or "no": what is, is. Meditation and contemplation are necessary because one

is on the level of acceptance and rejection, and the aim is in fact to go beyond acceptance and rejection. You want a support, do you not? The support that can take you beyond, to where the question of support or supportlessness no longer exists, that is the supportless support. What is expressible in words can certainly be attained. But He is THAT which is beyond words.

Inquirer: *I have read in books that some say they have to descend in order to act in the world. This seems to imply that although they are established in pure Being, they have to take the help of the mind when doing work. Just as a king, when acting the role of a sweeper, has for the time being to imagine he is a sweeper.*

Mātājī: In assuming a part, surely, there is no question of ascending or descending. Abiding in His own essential Being, He Himself plays various parts. But when you speak of ascending and descending—where is the state of pure Being. Can there be duality in that state? *Brahman* is One without a second. Though from your angle of vision, I grant, it does appear as you put it.

Inquirer: *You have explained this from the level of* ajñāna. *Now be pleased to speak from the level of the enlightened (*jñānin*)!*

Mātājī: (laughing). What you say now, I also accept. Here, (pointing to herself) nothing is rejected. Whether it is the state of enlightenment or of ignorance—everything is all right. The fact is that you are in doubt. But here there is no question of doubt. Whatever you may say, and from whatever level—is He, and He, and only He.

Question: *If this is so, is it of any use to ask you further questions?*

Mātājī: What is, IS. That doubts should arise is natural. But the wonder is, where THAT is, there is not even room for different stands to be taken. Problems are discussed, surely, for the purpose of dissolving doubts. Therefore it is useful to discuss. Who can tell when the veil will be lifted from your eyes? The purpose of discussion is to remove this ordinary sight; this

vision is no vision at all, for it is only temporary. Real vision is that vision where there is no such thing as the seer and the seen. It is eyeless—not to be beheld with these ordinary eyes, but with the eyes of wisdom. In that vision without eyes there is no room for "di-vision."

❦

Question: *What are the benefits to be derived from* hathayoga, *and what are its drawbacks?*

Mātājī: What does *hatha* mean? To do something by force. "Being" is one thing, and "doing" quite another. When there is "being," there will be the spontaneous manifestation of what is due to be manifested, owing to the life-force (*prāṇa*) functioning in a particular center of the body. On the other hand, if one practices *hathayoga* merely as a physical exercise, the mind will not be transformed in the very least.

Now, as to "doing": Sustained effort ends in effortless being; in other words, what has been attained by constant practice is finally transcended. Then comes spontaneity. Not until this happens can the utility of *hathayoga* be understood. When the physical fitness resulting from *hathayoga* is used as an aid to spiritual endeavor, it is not wasted. Otherwise it is not *yoga*, but *bhoga* (enjoyment). In effortless being lies the path to the Infinite. Unless *hathayoga* aims at the Eternal, it is nothing more than gymnastics. If in the normal course of the practice His touch is not felt, the *yoga* has been fruitless.

A competent teacher will accordingly either speed up the process or slow it down—just as a helmsman steers a boat with the rudder held firmly all the time. Without such direction *hathayoga* is not beneficial. He who would guide must have first-hand knowledge of everything that may occur at any stage, must see it with the perfect sharpness of direct perception. For is he not the physician of those on the path! Without the help of such a doctor, there is danger of injury.

Everything becomes smooth once the blessing of His touch has been felt. It is just as, when bathing in a river, one at first swims by one's own strength; but once caught in the current, whether a good swimmer or not, one is simply carried away. Therefore it is detrimental if this "touch" is not experienced. One must enter into the rhythm of one's true nature. Its revelation, acting as a flash of lightning, will attract one to it instantaneously, irresistibly; there comes a point where no further action is needed. So long as this contact has not been established, dedicate to God whatever inclinations or disinclinations you may have, and devote yourself to service, meditation, or contemplation—to anything of this kind.

Generally you perform your daily worship in the accustomed manner. If you feel the desire to practice some extra *japa* or meditation, it shows that you have caught a glimpse, however faint, and there is then hope that gradually the rhythm of your true nature may emerge. In this condition, the sense of "I" (*aham*) still persists, but this I is turned towards the Eternal, intent on union with Him. Whereas, actions done with a view to fame or distinction are of the ego (*ahaṁkāra*), and therefore obstacles, impediments.

Hathayoga can be harmful only if pure spiritual aspiration is lacking. When doing *āsana*s and the like, if you have found access to nature's own rhythm, you will see that everything proceeds smoothly and spontaneously. By what signs is this to be recognized? There is a sense of play, a deep delight, and the constant remembrance of the One. Indeed, this is not the outcome of the practice of worldly observances. What has been referred to here is that which can only become revealed spontaneously—of its own accord. This is why there is constant remembrance of the One: man's true nature flows towards God alone.

When the movement of your true nature sets in, then, because it is directed solely towards God, the knots of the heart will be unraveled. If during meditation you find perfectly correct *āsana*s forming of themselves—the spine becoming erect of its own accord—then you should know that the current of your *prāṇa* is turned towards the Eternal. Otherwise, when you are engaged in *japa*, the right flow will not come, and your back may begin to ache. Still, even this kind of *japa* is not without its effect, although its specific action is not experienced. In other words, the mind is willing but the body does not respond, and therefore you do not get the exhilaration that comes with the aroma of the divine presence.

To let the mind dwell on sense objects, still

further increases one's attachment to them. When intense interest in the supreme quest awakens, ever more time and attention will be given to religious thought, religious philosophy, the remembrance of God as immanent in all creation, until thereby every single knot is

untwisted. One is stirred by a deep yearning: "How can I find Him?" As a result of this, the rhythm of body and mind will grow steady, calm, serene.

Suppose some people go to bathe in the sea and make up their minds to swim ahead of everyone else; consequently they will have to look back. But for him whose one and only goal is the ocean itself, no one has remained for whose sake he looks back or is concerned; and then, what is to be, will be. Give yourself up to the wave, and you will be absorbed by the current; having dived into the sea, you do not return anymore. The Eternal Himself is the wave that floods the shore, so that you may be carried away. Those who can surrender themselves to this aim will be accepted by Him. But if your

attention remains directed towards the shore, you cannot proceed—after bathing you will return home. If your aim is the Supreme, the Ultimate, you will be led on by the movement of your true nature. There are waves that carry away, and waves that pull back. Those who can give themselves up, will be taken by Him. In the guise of the wave He holds out His hand and calls you come, Come, COME!

Question: *How can we benefit spiritually by action?*

Mātājī: By doing work for its own sake, engaging in *karmayoga* (the path of action). As long as a desire to distinguish oneself is lurking, it is *karmabhoga* (working for one's own satisfaction). One does the work and enjoys its fruit, because of the sense of prestige it brings.

Whereas, by relinquishing the fruit, it becomes *karmayoga*.

Question: *How is it possible to work without desire?*

Mātājī: By doing service with the feeling that one is serving the Supreme Being in everyone. The desire for God-realization is obviously not a desire in the ordinary sense. "I am Thy instrument; deign to work through this, Thy instrument." By regarding all manifestation as the Supreme Being, one attains to communion that leads to liberation. Whatever work is undertaken, let it be done with one's whole being and in the spirit: "Thou alone workest," so that there may be no opportunity for affliction, distress, or sorrow to creep in.

If for any reason there should arise even the least feeling of resentment, the action can no longer be described as being without attachment. Suppose, for example, after having accomplished by far the greater part of some work, you have to abandon it, and towards the end someone else takes it up, completes it, and gets the credit for having achieved the whole of the task. If you mind this even in the slightest degree, how can the work have really been done disinterestedly? Obviously it was not quite free from a desire for recognition.

Egoless work is full of beauty, for it is not prompted by a desire for self-gratification. So long as the knots that constitute the ego are not unraveled, even though you intend to act impersonally, you will get hurt, and this will produce a change in the expression of your eyes and face, and be apparent in your whole manner. To long, "let my heart be free from craving for results,"

is still a desire for a result. Nevertheless, by thus aspiring after selfless action there is hope of its coming to pass. A knot means resistance. Hence, so long as the ego persists, there will be clashes at times, even when impersonal work is attempted, because one is bound and therefore pulled in a certain direction.

Question: *So, until one has attained to perfect fulfillment, acting without a motive is an impossibility?*

Mātājī: When impersonal work is being carried out and watched as by a spectator, a deep joy surges up from within. If at that time the body gets hurt, even this becomes a source of

happiness. Nevertheless, this welling-up of joy is not identical with Self-realization. The thrill of delight brought about by impersonal work is His delight become one's own, His gladness felt as one's own; a stage has been reached where happiness is bound up with Him. In this condition, since one has lost interest in worldly pleasures, a great deal of work can be done in a perfect way; and even if despite one's utmost efforts some task has not succeeded fully, one does not feel disturbed. For everything has its place—here also His will prevails. Do you not see what an exquisite path this is! But the aforesaid holds good only when action is not tainted by a sense of possessiveness. However, even this state is by no means Self-realization. Why not? Whether with or without desire, it is work that is referred to here. Although done impersonally, the action still remains separate from the doer. So long as the duality of precept and action persists, one cannot possibly speak of Self-realization. The play of one who has attained to final consummation is entirely different from the work that has become selfless by effort.

The level of selfless action is quite different from the state of Self-realization. Yet, it must be said that action dedicated to God is not of the same order as work prompted by desire. The one is for the sake of union, which leads to enlightenment, the other for the sake of enjoyment which leads to further worldly experience. What alone is worthy to be called "action" is that action by which man's eternal union with God becomes revealed; all the rest is useless, unworthy of the name of action, no action at all. It is not a new kind of union which has to be established, but rather the union that exists throughout eternity is to be realized.

The sense of contentment experienced at the fulfillment of some worldly desire is relative happiness. This desire may be for one's wife, son, a relation, or any other person, and accordingly the fruit inherent in each particular action will be reaped. This is working for the sake of self-satisfaction (*bhoga*), not for the sake of union (*yoga*); it brings sorrow along with joy.

It is only on the level of the individual that pleasure and pain exist. In spite of attachment

to wife, husband, son or daughter, during spells of severe pain, when one tosses about in burning agony, is there room left for the thought of these loved ones? Does one not groan in a frenzy of self-pity? At that moment the delusion of family ties loses its hold, while the delusion of identifying oneself with the body reigns supreme. There exists oneself, that is why everything exists. From here, on this basis arises the alleged coming and going of the individual, its round of births and deaths.

———※❀❀———

In reply to a question concerning *dīkṣā* (initiation), Mātājī said:

He from whom one receives initiation, will bring one in touch with the levels up to where he himself has reached. Just as when one listens to a religious discourse, the speaker will communicate to the audience as much as lies in his power. In this there are two factors: the effect inherent in words of Truth, and the power of the speaker. Both are received, and if the recipient has outstanding capacity, supreme knowledge will dawn on him at the very instant he receives the instruction.

There are various kinds of initiation: by *mantra*, by touch, by a look, by instruction. Contact with a *mahātmā* does bear fruit. Everyone will benefit in proportion to his own receptivity and sincerity. There is also such a thing as special grace, by which unusual power to progress will be gained. On the other hand, there are cases where, in spite of actual contact, no infusion of power has taken place; one who commands power is able to control it—giving and taking depend on his will. When instruction frees a man from the knots that constitute the ego, this is called initiation by instruction. In this case the instruction has fulfilled its purpose instantaneously.

When *mantra dīkṣā* is given, the *mantra* is whispered into the initiate's ear, and the initiator will confer as much power as he himself

wields. If he is all-powerful he will, by his very touch or gaze, take the disciple to his final goal. But if he is not endowed with such supreme power, he can transmit to the initiate only whatever power he commands and guide him as far as he himself has reached. It is obvious that the *guru* can pass on only as much wealth as he possesses. If the person who has given the *mantra* has not reached the final goal and hence is still on the way, the disciple cannot progress any further unless the *guru* does.

However, the possibility of the disciple surpassing the *guru* exists; namely, when someone is initiated on the basis of his inner capacities and predispositions brought over from former births, his power to progress may thereby be stimulated to such an extent that he will be able to advance beyond the achievement of his *guru*. Here the initiate needs only just the amount of power conferred by the *dīkṣā* to take him to his goal. If a disciple has to rely entirely on the resources of his particular *guru*, he will have to move side by side with him. Furthermore, in the state in which one realizes that one's *guru* is the World-teacher and the World-teacher one's *guru*, one comes to know oneself as His servant, or as His very own Self, or as part of Him—any of these, depending on one's line of approach.

How is it that my *guru* may be said to be the World-teacher? For the simple reason that this is the status of a *guru*. Who for instance is a cook? The word "cook" surely does not denote the name of anyone in particular; it means one who can prepare food. Likewise, when the status of a *guru* becomes revealed, one understands that it has nothing to do with any person; the *guru* is none other than the World-teacher. If the power of the *guru* can become effective, there will be the realization of "Who am I?" He who is able to bestow that power is indeed a World-teacher. A *guru* is called he who, out of deep darkness, can reveal the hidden Truth. My *guru* exists in many forms as the *guru* of each and everyone, and everyone else's *guru* is in fact my *guru*. Now you see how the *guru* has become one.

Concerning the dedication of one's *japa* to one's *Iṣṭa* or *guru*, Mātājī said:

After doing *japa* one should dedicate it to the object of one's worship. If this is not done and it is stored by oneself, there is fear of its being lost, since one is not aware of the great value of what is in one's keeping. Just as when a priceless jewel is left in a small child's custody, he may throw the treasure away, not understanding how precious it is. Nevertheless, even by keeping the *japa* stored by oneself, one will gain something, but the full benefit of its accumulation will not be reaped. The whole and entire fruit of the *japa*, obtained by dedicating it to the supreme object of one's devotion, cannot be had if it is kept by oneself. For this reason *japa* should be offered to one's *Iṣṭa* or *guru*.

When one has acquired the necessary capacity, that which could not be understood formerly, is completely grasped. With age and wisdom, understanding comes in its fullness. By regularly offering one's *japa* to the *Iṣṭa*, one slowly and gradually comes to realize what the name is and He whose name one repeats; who one is; what Self-realization signifies. When all this is revealed, then the purpose of one's *japa* has been wholly fulfilled. Nobody can foretell at what particular instant this may occur; therefore, ever continue with your *sādhanā*.

Infinite are the *sādhanā*s, infinite the spiritual experiences, infinite is manifestation—and yet He is unmanifest. The nature of one's *japa* depends on one's particular line of approach. Why did I use the term "infinite"? The leaves of a tree are infinite in number, and although they are all of the same general pattern, yet there are countless variations within that pattern. Similarly, in the field of *sādhanā* also everything is infinite. Finally, when enlightenment occurs, this will be the end, and at that very instant He will be revealed in the midst of endless variety. For this reason persevere in the practice of *japa*. It will be carefully stored for you, as if kept safe-ly by your mother. The moment may come at any time, when you will realize the many in the One and the One in the many. When will the number of repetitions be completed, and what will then be found? That the name and the One whose name it is are indivisible; thus, what you have offered will come back to you.

In response to a question about the *mantra*, Mātājī said:

What indeed is a *mantra*? While one is bound by the idea of "I" and "you," and identifies oneself with the ego, the *mantra* represents the Supreme Being Himself in the guise of sound. Do you not see how beautifully certain syllables have been joined together in the *mahāvākya*s?[10] You think you are wholly bound, but this is only what your mind believes. That is why true knowledge can supervene at the very utterance of a word of power, which is composed merely of a few ordinary letters joined together. How mysterious and intimate is the relation between those words and the immutable *Brahman*! Take for example, the *Śabda Brahman*:[11] merely by the *Śabda* (sound) one becomes established in the Self. Look, the ocean is contained in the drop, and the drop in the ocean. What else is the spark, if not a particle of fire—of Him, who is knowledge supreme.

It is the notion of "you" and "I" by which your mind has been held captive all along; you should understand that the combination of sounds which has the power to free you from this bondage is the one to be used. Verily, it is through sound that one penetrates into Silence; for He is manifest in all forms without exception. Indeed, everything is possible in the state that is beyond knowledge and ignorance.

[10] The "great sayings" that summarize the wisdom of the Upaniṣads, e.g. "*Tat tvam asi*" (That thou art).

[11] Sound *Brahman*; the eternal sound that is the first manifestation of undifferentiated *Brahman* and lies at the root of all subsequent creation.

So long as you are not finally established in that supreme knowledge, you all dwell in the realm of waves and sound. There are sounds that cause the mind to turn outwards, and others that draw it within. But the sounds that tend outwards are also connected with those that lead inwards. Therefore, because of their inter-relation, there may, at some auspicious moment, occur that perfect union, which is followed by the great Illumination, the revelation of what is. Why should not this be possible, since He is ever Self-revealed?

———⊰⊱———

Question: *In* Vicār Sāgara[12] *we read of a certain Rāja's minister, named Bharju, who in spite of having gained knowledge of Truth, was still not free of illusion. I do not understand how, when a thing has become revealed, the question of its obscuration can still arise.*

Mātājī: One thing is the full and final realization of unveiled light; but quite another is a realization due to some cause, in which the possibility of its being obscured again, still exists. At the time when the play of *sādhanā* was being manifested through this body, it could clearly perceive these various possibilities.

You should understand that if a veil of ignorance has been burnt or dissolved, as it were, the seeker will, for a certain period of time, have unobstructed vision. Afterwards it becomes blurred again. All the same—what will be the result of such a glimpse? Ignorance will have become less dense, and true knowledge gained greater prominence; in other words, by the momentary lifting of the veil, the individual's bonds will have been loosened. In this condition there is a semblance of the attainment of real knowledge; in fact, it is also a state of achievement, although quite different from the state of final Self-realization. By the power of the *guru* the veil has here been suddenly dissolved or consumed. But there is a realization,

after which the possibility of its being obscured again by a reappearance of the veil of ignorance, simply cannot occur: this is true and final Self-realization. Lightning comes in a flash, but the light of day continues steadily.

Question: *How can anything occur that is not mentioned in the* Śāstras?

Mātājī: To expound reincarnation, *karma,* and similar doctrines, is mainly the work of the *Śāstras.* Whether anything may occur that is not mentioned in them—just remember that He is infinite! Out of your union with this Infinity spring your actions, feelings, and thoughts, at the present time or in the future, in whatever form He may be pleased to assume. This you may not be able to learn from *Śāstras.* Nevertheless, the *Śāstras* are also infinite. Oh, how beautiful is the law of God's creation! Do you not know the feeling of delight, of deep bliss, when in a new way you experience a glimpse of Him, the eternally new!

Just consider: The Infinite is contained in the finite, and the finite in the Infinite; the Whole in the part and the part in the Whole. This is so, when one has entered the great stream. He who attains and that which is attained are one and the same. It is not merely a matter of imagination; through ever fresh channels He is perceived in ever new forms. Having entered that unbroken stream, it is only natural that *yoga,* the hidden union of the individual with the All, should become *mahāyoga* (supreme union).

Look, everything is contained in the *Śāstras,* and yet not everything. Imagine that you are traveling by train to Dehradun. On your journey you will pass through large stations, through towns and villages. Everyone of these has been indicated in the guide-book. But what is seen between the different stations, can it all be described in full detail? The trees and plants, the animals and birds, the tiny little ants that are met with on the way, could all these be delineated? Looked at from this point of view, not everything has been written down in the *Śāstras.* Infinite is the diversity of creation, infi-

---

[12] A work on *Vedānta* written in Hindi.

nite are its modes of being, its changing movements and static states, revealed at every single instant. Furthermore, it is quite certain that Reality is beyond speech and thought. Only that which can be expressed in words is being said. But what cannot be put into language, is indeed That which IS.

The study of Scriptures and similar texts—provided it does not become an obsession—can be an aid towards the grasping of Truth. So long as what has been read has not become one's own experience, that is to say, has not been assimilated into one's own being, it has not fulfilled its purpose. A seed that is merely held in the hand cannot germinate: it must develop into a plant and bear fruit in order to reveal its full possibilities.

When at certain stages you have realizations, these will of course be within the confines of your own particular line of approach. In the event of complete realization, can such a thought as, "it has not been mentioned in the *Śāstra*s," have any meaning? If someone has a doubt about something because it is not contained in the *Śāstra*s, can he have attained to the goal of his pilgrimage? Affirmation and negation are of significance only while one is yet on the way, for there are paths without number, and they cannot be limited to what has been laid down in the *Śāstra*s. Where the Infinite is in question, the diversity of approaches is equally infinite, and likewise are the revelations along these paths, of endless variety. Is it not said: "There are as many doctrines as there are sages"?

Later someone declared:

Self-realization cannot be attained by the repetition of any name whatsoever, but only by understanding the processes of the mind. Every problem that arises in the mind has to be thought out and understood in all its implications, and in this way dissolved. If a person be incapable of doing this himself, he may seek the help of someone else, no matter whom. However, by this, the relationship that is considered permanent between guru *and disciple will not be established. Who essentially is the* guru, *since all are one!*

Mātājī: Pitājī, when this teaching is given, do not those who are trying to put it into practice automatically accept him who expounds it as their *guru*?

The Person Addressed: *No, for when their problems have been solved, all are again on an equal footing.*

Mātājī: Quite so. Thus we are also told that after the *guru* has given *saṁnyāsa*, he prostrates himself at full length before the disciple, in order to demonstrate that there is no difference between *guru* and disciple; for both are indeed one.

By concentrating on the problems that arise in the mind, it may be possible to undo the knots that constitute the ego. For this reason the above method is not in contradiction to any other. What has been said about being on an equal footing is also right, for in this world people have to assist and teach one another in many walks of life; therefore it can be truly said that everybody is a *guru*. From one point of view one may call one's *guru* every person from whom one has learnt something, no matter how little. But the real *guru* is He whose teaching helps one towards Self-realization.

Suppose a person is walking in the dark and a dog suddenly starts barking furiously quite close to him. What can be the matter? The man switches on his torch and finds himself confronted with a big poisonous snake. By taking great care he is now able to elude the venomous fangs. Will the dog in this case have to be called his *guru* or not? One may certainly object to it, for the dog did not bark for the purpose of making the man aware. But He who bestows awareness may appear in the guise of a dog.

Question: *If the Real remains what it is what then do ascent and descent mean?*

Mātājī: What you say represents a particular viewpoint of the world. Where the Ultimate, the Supreme, is, the question you ask is impossible. On a certain plane, descent and ascent exist. It is you who say: "God descends." On the other hand, there is no such thing as descent: where He is, there He remains, and all possibilities are contained in Him.

The beauty of it is that man's very nature is to long for Reality, Supreme Wisdom, Divine Joy; as it is his nature to return home when the play is over. The stage of the play is His, the play His as well, and so are those who take part in it, friends and fellow-beings—everything is He alone.

To long for the cessation of want is your very nature, and to explore and penetrate to the root of whatever you perceive. When you buy clothes you choose durable material, which will not wear out quickly; even this is an indication of your innate tendency to seek the everlasting.

It is your nature to crave for the revelation of That which is, for the Eternal, for Truth, for limitless Knowledge. This is why you do not feel satisfied with the evanescent, the untrue, with ignorance and limitation. Your true nature is to yearn for the revelation of what you ARE.

Concerning the nature of duality and of the state beyond duality, Mātājī said:

He alone IS—so there is no question of acceptance or denial. Did He ever come into being that there could be a possibility of accepting or denying Him? He was never born. According to one angle of vision, it is true that this world does not exist, that Truth is found by eliminating name and form; on the other hand, name and form are made up of the *akṣara*,[13]

---

[13] A play on words: *akṣara* means "indestructible," and also "letters of the alphabet."

of that which is indestructible. But in essence, THAT is Truth. The appearance of the phenomenal world (due to erroneous perception) and its disappearance (due to right knowledge) are ultimately one and the same thing: both are He. Then again there is no question of clearing up error, for there is only He, the one ground of all. With Him as one's goal, the error that there is such a thing as error has to be uprooted. Talk of this kind is all just by way of helping one to understand.

Whatever anyone does, belongs to the realm of death, of ceaseless change. Nothing can be excluded. In the shape of death art Thou, and in the form of desire; Thou art becoming and Thou art being, differentiation as well as identity—for Thou art infinite, without end. Thou it is who roamest in the disguise of nature. From whatever standpoint an assertion may be made, I never object to it. For He is all in all, He alone is—the One with form and without form. In your present condition your divine essence cannot be revealed. When a roof is being built, it is a law that whatever materials are hammered into it, must remain there. No matter how much time it may require, the roof must be made solid. Likewise, (no simile is ever complete) you identify yourself with any line of work in which you are expert, believing it to be your real nature. So far so good; but where is the whole of your being, which is with form as well as formless? Therefore you should reflect: What is it that has to be attained? You will have to become conscious of your Self in its entirety. Nay, to become fully conscious is not enough; you will have to rise beyond consciousness and unconsciousness. The revelation of THAT is what is wanted. You will have to go on discriminating and make a sustained effort to convince your mind of the fact that *japa*, meditation, and all other spiritual exercises, have for purpose your awakening. On this pilgrimage one must never slacken: effort is what counts! Thus one should try ever to remain engrossed in this endeavor— it must be woven into one's very being, one has

to be fused with one's Self. It is Thou that criest out helplessly in distress, and it is Thou Thyself that art the way and the goal. In order that this may be revealed, man must employ his intelligence vigorously and unceasingly.

A tree is watered at its roots. Man's root is the brain, where his reasoning power, his intellect is constantly at work. Through *japa*, meditation, the perusal of Scriptures, and similar practices, one progresses towards the goal. Hence man should bind himself and, fixing his gaze on the One, advance along the path. Whatever ties, bonds, or restraints he imposes upon himself, should have for aim the supreme goal of life. With untrammeled energy one must forge ahead towards the discovery of one's own Self.

Whether one takes the path of devotion, where the "I" is lost in the "Thou," or the path of Self-inquiry, in search of the true "I"—it is He alone who is found in the "Thou" as well as in the "I."

Why should one's gaze be fixed, while treading the path? The gaze is He and the "why" is also He. Whatever is revealed or hidden anywhere, in any way, is "Thou," is "I." Negation, just as affirmation, are equally "Thou"—the One. You will be able to grasp this fully only when you find everything within yourself; in other words, in the state where there is nothing but the Self. This is why you should direct your gaze towards the Eternal while on the Way. Where you see limitation, even this is a manifestation of the Limitless, the Infinite. In essence it is none other than your own Self. So long as this fact has not been revealed, how can one speak of full realization—complete, perfect, all-comprehensive—call it what you will! Then again, how can the question of perfection or imperfection, of completeness or incompleteness, still arise in such a state of fulfillment?

Question: *You say all moments are contained in the one supreme moment. I cannot understand this.*

Mātājī: In reality there is nothing but the one moment all along. Just as one single tree contains numberless trees, innumerable leaves, infinite movement, and untold static states, so does one moment contain an infinite number of moments, and within all these countless moments lies the one single moment. Look, there is motion as well as rest in that supreme moment. Why then should the revelation of the moment be spoken of? Because, misled by your perception of differences, you think of yourself and of each and every creature or object in the world as being apart from one another. This is why, for you, separateness exists. The sense of separateness in which you are caught, that is to say, the moment of your birth, has determined your nature, your desires and their fulfillment, your development, your spiritual search—everything. Consequently, the moment of your birth is unique, the moment of your mother's birth is also unique, and so is that of your father's; and the nature and temperament of each of the three is unique.

In accordance with your own particular line of approach, each one of you must seize the time, the moment that will reveal to you the eternal relationship by which you are united to the Infinite: this is the revelation of supreme union. Supreme union signifies that the whole universe is within you, and you are in it; and further, there will be no occasion to speak of a universe. Whether you say it exists or does not exist, or that it can neither be said to exist or not to exist, or even beyond that—as you please. What matters is that He should stand revealed, be it in whatever form.

At that "moment," at that point of time—when it is found—you will know your Self. To know your Self implies the revelation (at that very same instant) of what your father and mother in reality are, and not only your father and mother, but the entire universe. It is that moment which links up the whole of creation. For to know yourself does not mean to know your body only; it signifies the full revelation of

That which eternally is—the Supreme Father, Mother, Beloved, Lord and Master—the Self. Just as by receiving one seed, you have potentially received an infinite number of trees, so must you capture the one supreme moment, the realization of which will leave nothing unrealized.

———

Someone declared that *Vedānta* and *bhakti* were two entirely different doctrines or lines of approach.

Mātājī: Where doctrines are, there all-inclusiveness cannot be. What is emphasized from one point of view will be rejected from another. But where is the state in which difference and non-difference have ceased to exist? Some maintain that the conception of Rādhā-Kṛṣṇa[14] is completely Vedāntic, for Kṛṣṇa cannot be without Rādhā, nor Rādhā without Kṛṣṇa—they are two in one and one in two.

Inquirer: *It is said that God's eternal* līlā *is based on duality.*

Mātājī: The assumption of duality is also within Oneness; some advocate this opinion. They say that even in the midst of this *līlā*, Oneness remains unimpaired. In *Vedānta* too, duality is out of the question. Although duality appears to manifest itself before the eyes of the *bhakta*, nevertheless, here also there is nothing but Oneness. If one does not view things through the spectacles of the *bhakta*, this cannot be grasped. Seen from his angle of vision, it appears thus.

Suppose when giving initiation the *guru* instructs the disciple to practice the formal worship of Rādhā-Kṛṣṇa, and to regard himself as the servant, and Rādhā-Kṛṣṇa as his Master. By regularly engaging in worship and service of this kind, the following development may take place: First of all one feels that the room in which the worship is being performed has to be consecrated to the Deity, and He has to be wor-

[14] The union of Lord Kṛṣṇa and his consort Rādhā.

shipped with lights, incense, etc. (*āratī*). As one continues day after day to carry out these acts of worship, one begins to question: "Is my Lord as small as this little image? Does He dwell only in my shrine-room and nowhere else?" By performing His service one gradually comes to feel that all is His. This feeling grips one and spreads like an infectious disease. Someone once said: "Do not venture near Ānandamayī Mā, there are small-pox germs around her." (Laughter). Single-minded devotion engenders deep thought, which expresses itself in action. The Lord's light descends on the devotee, His power awakens in him and, as a result, profound inner inquiry blossoms forth.

Then follows a stage, where it happens that one may have a vision of the Beloved—for instance, while scrubbing the vessels used for *pūjā*, or one may lie asleep and see Him standing near one's bed. Look, at first one believed the Lord to be present in one's prayer-room, but by and by one is able to perceive Him here and there. At a further stage, not anymore in particular places, but wherever one turns one's eyes: He is seen sitting in trees, standing in water; He is perceived within animals and birds. However, even here one's vision of Him is not uninterrupted.

Then comes a time when the Beloved does not leave one anymore; wherever one may go, He is ever by one's side and His presence constantly felt. At an earlier stage one perceived Him within all objects; but now He is not seen *within* the objects anymore, for there is nothing but He alone. Trees, flowers, the water, and the land—everything is the Beloved, and only He. Every form, every mode of being, every expression—whatever exists is He, there is none beside Him. It may occur that a *sādhikā* continues in this state for the rest of his life.

If everything is the Lord and nothing but He, then one's body must also be He—the One Existence. In this state, when one is deeply absorbed in *dhyāna*, no physical activity—be it the performance of ritual or acts of service—is

possible. For He alone IS. One no longer exists apart from Him. What would the Vedāntists say? "There is only one *Brahman* without a second." Nevertheless, for some who have attained to this condition, the relationship between the Lord and His servant remains and is felt thus: "He is the Whole and I am part of Him, and yet there is only the one Self." If the *Brahman* is described as the splendor of Kṛṣṇa's body—why should one object? Verily, everything is identical, undivided. To realize this means to be immersed completely into the ocean of Oneness.

After this has been accomplished, one can again do *pūjā* and service, for the relationship between Master and servant persists. Mahābīr[15] said: "He and I are one; yet He is the Whole and I am part of Him; He is the Master, I am His servant." If, after the one Self has been realized, the relationship of a servant to his Master still continues, why should anyone object? At first this was the path to one's goal. After realization it is He, the One, who serves. This is real service.

Question: *After having realized the Oneness of all, due to what need or imperfection does it become necessary again to worship a particular deity?*

Mātājī: In that state there is no need or imperfection.

Inquirer: *But then it cannot be service or worship as we understand them!*

Mātājī: You may call it anything. The point is this: Śukadeva was a liberated being; why then did he relate the *Śrīmad Bhāgavata*?[16] The need or imperfection that prompted one to serve and worship at the initial stage, has no place here.

The Vedāntists discard one thing after another, saying "*neti, neti*" ("not this, not this"). Indeed, you see a beautiful flower, and a few days later it has been reduced to dust; therefore

---

[15] Literally "great hero." An epithet of Hanumān, the supreme devotee of Rāma, *avatāra* of Viṣṇu. See further p. 69.

[16] A chronicle of the ten *avatāra*s of Viṣṇu, related by the the saint Śukadeva Goswami.

what they say is perfectly true. What is subject to change will most certainly change. On the other hand, expressed in the terms of those who believe in the reality of name and form, one may say: "All names are Thy Name, all forms Thy Form." Here name and form are also real. Again, it may be argued: "What is bound by change is the world. By persevering in the practice of discrimination, one finally becomes established in the one Reality." When there is only the one ocean—nothing but water—one cannot see oneself as separate from the all. This is full immersion. Nevertheless, if outwardly or inwardly, even so much as a hair has remained

dry, it signifies that complete immersion has not yet occurred. When a seed has been fried it can never sprout again. Just so, after realizing Oneness, you may do anything—it no longer contains the seed of *karma*. Look, by intense devotion as well as by Vedāntic discrimination one has arrived at the one Essence. Does then "to merge into IT" mean to become stone-like? Not so, indeed! For form, variety, manifestation are nothing but THAT.

The characteristic features of each person's particular path will of course be preserved; yet, what is attained is the One, in which no doubt, no uncertainty can survive. In fact, what is there to be attained? We *are* THAT—eternal Truth. Because we imagine that it has to be experienced, realized, it remains apart from us. On some levels this point of view is valid, but on others it is not. The Eternal ever IS. What is styled "the veil of ignorance" signifies continual motion. Motion means change, incessant transformation. Yet again, no change takes place where there is non-action in action. For such a one duality does not exist; who then eats, and what can he eat? In this state, how can there be theories or disputes? If someone argues that, since a certain person speaks, he cannot have attained to this state,—what does he speak and to whom? Who is the one to whom he speaks? This is so when full realization has come about.

Having realized the one Self, and that there is nothing outside of It, one knows that the image one has worshipped is THAT in a particular form. Having found Reality, one perceives it in this particular guise: the deity I adored is none other than the one Self, the *Brahman*—there is no second. Thus, the One is the Lord I worshipped. When one has dived into the depth of the sea, water is known to be He in one form. The aspirant who advances along the path of *bhakti* will, when he has attained to the vision of his Master, become a true servant. The methods of "not this, not this" and "this is Thou, this is Thou" lead to the one goal. By proceeding in one direction It is reached, and by taking the other direction, one also arrives at the very same goal. Those who follow the path of surrender to *Śakti*, the Divine Energy, and those who worship the image of Śiva, both must finally attain to the one *Śakti*, the one Śiva. It may be asked, why there cannot be one and the same path for

all? Because He reveals Himself in infinite ways and forms—verily, the One is all of them. In that State there is no "why." Quarrels and disputes exist merely on the way. With whom is one to quarrel? Only while still on the way is it possible to have disputes and differences of opinion.

Equality, Oneness must come and become a permanent state. Having achieved it, if someone says: "I am renouncing liberation," or "I am giving up the worship of my *Iṣṭa*"—even though he may give it up, nothing will be lost; for in this condition there is neither renouncing nor retaining. "*Devo bhutva devam yajet*" ("Only by becoming identified with the Lord, can one worship Him"). If, after Self-realization, after one's essential Being has revealed Itself, one still performs the worship of one's particular deity, it means engaging in one's own worship. This is *līlā*.

––––––––✦––––––––

Question: *Please explain the nature of worldly and divine happiness.*

Mātājī: Divine happiness is pure, unalloyed bliss, happiness in its own right.

Question: *But surely, there is happiness in the world too!*

Mātājī: Then why do you make this remark?

Question: *Why do people run after material happiness?*

Mātājī: You know this happiness from experience, and hence your question. But God is gracious and makes you see that this so-called happiness is not happiness. He kindles discontent and anguish in you, which is due to the want of communion with the Divine. Worldly happiness is derived from the countless manifestations of God. People talk and marvel about those who renounce the world, but in actual fact it is you yourself who have renounced everything. What is this "everything"? God! Leaving Him aside, everyone is literally practicing

supreme renunciation. (Laughter). It is only natural that the sense of want should awaken. Even in the midst of comforts and pleasures one feels homesick in a foreign land. There is distress even in happiness, one's possessions are not really one's own—this is what He causes man to feel. It is said, is it not, that on being hit one recovers one's senses, one learns by receiving blows.

When He manifests Himself as worldly happiness, one does not feel contented, for along with it He appears as the sense of want. But divine happiness, even the tiniest particle of a grain of it, never leaves one again; and when one attains to the essence of things and finds one's Self—this is supreme happiness. When it is found, nothing else remains to be found; the sense of want will not awaken anymore, and the heart's torment will be stilled for ever. Do not be satisfied with fragmentary happiness, which is invariably interrupted by shocks and blows of fate; but become complete, and having attained to perfection, be YOURSELF.

Question: *Why does one not remember one's former lives?*

Mātājī: Through ignorance; there is no knowledge, due to the veil that hides it.

Question: *But why should there be a veil? After the body dies, the mind continues, also one is able to remember what has happened today and yesterday; why therefore should the events of one's past lives be forgotten?*

Mātājī: Having entered the kingdom of forgetting, everything is forgotten; this world is the abode of non-remembrance.

Question: *Why should so very much be forgotten? A small portion might at least be remembered!*

Mātājī: You say, do you not, that the Lord Buddha talked about the events of five hundred of his previous lives. Can you recall everything that you experienced in your present birth, from your childhood until now? You die at every instant without being aware of it. At present you are neither an infant, nor a child, nor a youth. No sooner is a baby born than he starts of his own accord to drink his mother's milk, and when he has drunk, he feels happy and satisfied; by this he has already given full testimony of former births. Now also, whenever your hunger has been appeased, you experience a similar sense of well-being and contentment as you did in your early childhood, although you do not recollect what you felt at that time.

A *yogī* can perceive the impressions of a great number of past lives. One may see the events of thousands of one's former births, but when the realization has come of what creation with its ascending and descending currents in reality is, what will he see then? He will see, and also not see: and neither will he not see, nor see. Where everything that exists is revealed in its fullness—this is called Self-revelation, THAT Itself, the Self-luminous One—call it what you will.

Suppose you are able to visualize a few of your previous lives: your vision is limited by number. If you recollect the history of your former births, it means that you know only the course of your own individual lives, in their own particular times and places. But you are not aware of your various movements and static states in the whole universe. You see "the many"; how will you go beyond this multiplicity? By finding your Self in the many. Who is that Self? He, and none but He. So long as He, the Self, has not been revealed, you are imprisoned within the boundary; boundary means ignorance, and therefore there is forgetting.

Question: *Surely, one who has become established in the Self will naturally forget the world?*

Mātājī: Look, if there were no veil of ignorance for the individual, how could God's *līlā* be carried on? When acting a part one must forget oneself; the *līlā* could not proceed without the covering veil of ignorance. Consequently it is but natural that the veil should be there. So, the world is the perception by the senses of what is projected. To be a separate individual means to be bound, and that which binds is the veil of ignorance; here is the clue to the forgetting about which you asked.

When you speak of previous births you intuitively feel: "Was there ever a time when I was not?" It is you who speak in terms of "before" and "after," since you are confined within the realm of time. But really there is no question of "in time" and "out of time"; nor of day and night, "before" and "after." So long as one remains enslaved by time, there will be birth and death. Actually, there is no such thing as rebirth. Still, at some stage the memory of previous lives will most certainly occur, but what is the significance of "before" and "after," since I exist throughout eternity?

All that exists anywhere in the world, be it trees and plants, insects, reptiles, or any other living thing—their birth is indeed your birth, and their death your death. On the level where everything is contained within you and you are present in everything, there is only the One, and He alone.

⟞⟝

Question: *If someone advances along the path of* advaita, *will he acquire* vibhūtis *(supernormal powers)?*

Mātājī: If you speak of a *sādhikā* who aspires to the state of unqualified Oneness, then, even if supernormal powers come to him, he will not accept them. Whereas the aspirant who worships God with form and attributes, will accept whatever psychic or super-psychic powers are granted to him, regarding them as manifestations of the One. Such powers are bound to be developed in the course of *sādhanā*, since they represent the fruit of one's efforts. The word *vibhūti* signifies the various manifestations of the All-Pervading (*Vibhū*). For this reason it is only natural and certain that *vibhūti*s should come. The aspirant must however take care not

to be possessed by these powers, because his progress would then be arrested at that stage.

⟞⟝

Question: *Is grace (*ahetuka kṛpā*) without cause or reason?*

Mātājī: Certainly; for grace is by its very nature beyond cause or reason. When working, one reaps the fruit of one's actions. If, for instance, you serve your father and he, being pleased with your service, gives you a present, this would be called the fruit of action. One does something and receives something in return. But the eternal relationship that by nature exists between father and son, does surely not depend on any action. The Supreme Father, Mother, and Friend—verily, God is all of these. Consequently, how can there be a cause or reason for His grace? You are His, and in whatever way He may draw you to Him, it is for the sake of revealing Himself to you. The desire to find Him that awakens in man—who has instilled it into you? Who is it that makes you work for its fulfillment?

Thus you should try to arrive at the understanding that everything originates from Him. Whatever power, whatever skill you possess,—why, even you yourself—from where does everything arise? And does it not all have for purpose the finding of Him, the destroying of the veil of ignorance? Whatever exists has its origin in Him alone. Are you master even of a single breath? To whatever small degree He makes you feel that you have freedom of action, if you understand that this freedom has to be used to aspire after the realization of Him, it will be for your good. But if you regard yourself as the doer, and God as being far away, and if, owing to His apparent remoteness, you work for the gratification of your desires, it is wrong action. You should look upon all things as manifestations of Him. When you recognize the existence of God, He will reveal Himself to you as compassionate, or gracious, or merciful,

in accordance with your attitude towards Him at the time. Just as, for example, to the humble He becomes the Lord of the humble.

When a *sādhikā* starts worshipping an image of his Beloved, he will in the course of his practice attain to a condition in which the form

of his Beloved is beheld, wherever his eyes may fall. Next he comes to realize: "All other deities are contained in my Beloved." He sees that everyone's Lord, in fact all things, are contained in his own *Iṣṭa*, and that his *Iṣṭa* also dwells in all deities, as indeed, in everything. The *sādhikā* comes to feel: "As my Lord resides within me, so He, who is present within everyone else, is truly the same Lord. In water and on land, in trees, shrubs, and creepers—everywhere in the whole universe abides my Beloved. Further, all the various forms and modes of being that we behold, are they not expressions of my Beloved? For there is none save Him. He is smaller than the smallest, and greater than the greatest."

Actuated by your various inborn tendencies, you each worship a different deity. The true progress in one's spiritual experience depends on the sincerity and intensity of one's aspiration. The measure of a person's spiritual advance will be reflected in the manifestations that are vouchsafed to him of his *Iṣṭa*, who will by no means remain inaccessible or separate from His devotee, but let Himself be contacted in an infinite variety of ways. Conditioned though you be, you will find the All within you, and on the other hand, be able to grasp that your own innate tendencies are also part of this All. What has been said here, represents one point of view. You cannot dissociate yourself from the Whole.

The multifarious kinds of beasts, birds, men and so forth—what are they all? What are these varieties of shapes, of modes of being, what is the essence within them? What really are these ever-changing forms? Gradually, slowly, because you are rapt in the contemplation of your "Beloved," He becomes revealed to you in every one of them; not even a grain of sand is excluded. You realize that water, earth, plants, animals, birds, human beings, are nothing but forms of your Beloved. Some experience it in this manner—realization does not come to everyone in the same way. There are infinite possibilities. Consequently, the specific path along which—

for any particular person—the Universal will reveal itself in its boundlessness, remains concealed from the average individual.

What you have read in the *Śrīmad Bhāgavata* about the universal body of the Lord, which comprises all things—trees, flowers, leaves, hills, mountains, rivers, oceans, and so forth,—a time will come, must come, when one actually perceives this all-pervading universal form of the One. The variety of His shapes and guises is infinite, uncountable, without end. "He who is multi-shaped, who constantly creates and destroys these His forms, He is the One whom I adore." To the degree that you grow in the ever fuller and wider recognition of this truth, you will realize your oneness with each of these numberless forms.

In this connection it must be said that, if one wants to find Truth, everything will have to be realized as it is in its own place, without choosing one thing rather than another. It is a kingdom without end, in which even what is discerned as non-existence is equally an expression of the One. In the purely spiritual world, all forms—whatever they be—are ever eternal. Therefore, simultaneously and in the same place, there is non-existence as well as existence, and also neither non-existence nor existence—and more of the kind if you can proceed further! Look at the ever-changing world, where what exists at one moment is non-existent the next, where being is continually entering into non-being—who then is this non-being? Even the non-existent exists.

Very well, just as ice is nothing but water, so the Beloved is without form, without quality, and the question of manifestation does not arise. When this is realized, one has realized one's Self. For, to find the Beloved is to find my self, to discover that God is my very own, wholly identical with myself, my innermost Self, the Self of my Self. Then, according to the exigence of time and circumstance, various possibilities may take effect; as, for example, the revelation of *mantra*s and even of the entire Vedas by the

ancient *ṛṣi*s who were seers of *mantra*s. All this will occur in consonance with the individual *karma* and inner disposition of the person concerned.

It is the perception of the world, based upon the identification of yourself with body and mind, that has all along been the source of your bondage. A time will come, when this kind of perception will give way before the awakening of universal consciousness, which will reveal itself as an aspect of supreme knowledge. When this knowledge of the essence of things has come, what happens to the Essence Itself? Ponder over this! When insight into form and the formless dawns in its boundlessness, everything will be uprooted. On transcending the level where form, diversity, manifestation exist, one enters into a state of formlessness. What can this be called? Godhood, the *Paramātmā* (Supreme Spirit) Himself. As the individual self becomes gradually freed from all fetters, which are nothing but the veil of ignorance, it realizes its oneness with the Supreme Spirit and becomes established in its own essential Being.

Well, now suppose a man follows his own specific path, which happens to be the worship of a deity. Who actually is present as that particular deity? Certainly the One, who is the formless Self! Consequently, just as the formless Self is He, so is the concrete object of worship. One who, by the method of *Vedānta*, has become fully established in the Self, may also find the Supreme Reality in the *vigraha* (literally "form"; a consecrated image), just as water is contained in ice. He will then come to see that all *vigraha*s are really spiritual forms of the One. He alone is water as well as ice. What is there in ice? Nothing but water. According to *dvaitādvaita*,[17] duality and non-duality are both facts; expressed from this position, there is form as well as freedom from form. Again, when saying there are both duality and non-duality, where does this kind of statement hold good? There is certainly a level where difference and non-difference are perceived simultaneously. In very truth, He is as much in difference as He is in non-difference. Look, from the worldly point of view, one quite obviously assumes that there are differences. The very fact that you are endeavoring to find your Self shows that you accept difference, that, in the manner of the world, you think of yourself as separate. From this standpoint difference undoubtedly exists. But then the world is inevitably heading towards destruction (*nāśa*), since it is not the Self (*nā Sva*), not He (*na Śa*). It cannot last for ever. Yet, who is it that appears even in the

guise of the ephemeral? Ponder over this! Well then, what goes and what comes? Behold, it is movement as that of the sea (*samudra*), He expressing Himself (*sva mudra*). The waves are but the rising and the falling, the undulation of the water, and it is water that forms into waves (*taranga*)—limbs of His own body (*tār anga*)—water in essence. What is it that makes the same substance appear in different forms, as water, ice, waves? This again is asked from a particular plane of consciousness. Reflect and see how much of it you can grasp! No simile is ever valid in all respects.

The aforesaid implies that He eternally manifests, displaying form and quality, and yet is without form and quality; and still further, that the question of attributes and attributelessness cannot arise since there is solely the One-without-a-second. You speak of the Absolute as Truth, Knowledge, Infinity. In pure *advaita* no question of form, quality, or predication—be it affirmative or negative—can possibly arise. When you say: "This indeed is He and that also

---

[17] Literally "dualistic non-dualism." A school of *Vedānta*.

is He," you have limited yourself by the word "also," and as a result assume the separateness of the thing referred to. In the One there can be no "also." The state of supreme Oneness cannot be described as "THAT," and also something "other than THAT." In the attributeless *Brahman* there can be no such thing as quality or absence of quality; there is only the Self alone.

Suppose you hold that He is with quality, embodied. When you become wholly centered in the particular form you adore, then formlessness does not exist for you—this is one state. There is another state where He appears with attributes as well as without. There is yet another state where difference as well as non-difference exist—both being inconceivable—where He is quite beyond thought. This and all that has been said above, is within the supreme state, of which it is said that, even though the Whole is taken from the Whole, the Whole remains unimpaired. There can be no additions and no subtractions; the wholeness of the Whole remains unaltered. Whatever line you may follow represents a particular aspect of it. Each method has its own *mantra*s, its own methods, its beliefs and disbeliefs—to what purpose? To realize Him, your own Self. Who or what is this Self? Depending on your orientation, you find Him, who is your own Self, in the relation of a perfect servant to his Master, of a part to the Whole, or simply as the one Self (*Ātmā*).

Very well, the many creeds and sects serve the purpose that He may bestow Himself on Himself[18] along various channels—each has its own beauty—and that He may be discovered as immanent, revealing Himself in countless ways, in all shapes, and in the formless. As the path, He attracts each person to a particular line, in harmony with his inner dispositions and tendencies. The One is present in each sect, even though in some cases there appears to be conflict among them, due to the limitations of the ego. This body, however, does not exclude any-

thing. He who follows one particular creed or sect, will have to proceed right up to the point where all that it stands for is known to him in its entirety. When advancing along one line, in other words, when adhering to one particular religion, faith, or creed—which you conceive as distinct and as conflicting with all the others— you will, first of all, have to realize the perfection to which its Founder points and then, what is beyond will of itself become revealed to you.

What has just been explained, is applicable in the case of each of the various sects; yet it is of course true that, if one remains satisfied with whatever can be achieved by following one line, the goal of human life has not been attained. What is required is a realization that will uproot conflict and divergence of opinion, that is complete and free from inherent antagonism. If it be anything less than that, it means that one's experience is partial, incomplete. In the event of true realization, one can have no quarrel with anyone—one is fully enlightened as to all faiths and doctrines, and sees all paths as equally good. This is absolute and perfect realization. So long as there is dissension, one cannot speak of attainment. Nevertheless, one should undoubtedly have firm faith in one's *Iṣṭa* and pursue one's chosen path with constancy and single-mindedness.

[18] A play upon words: *Sampradāya*, religious sect; *sama*, fully; *pradān kora*, to give, to offer.

APPENDIX I
Further Discourses on Spiritual Practice[1]

Question: *How can the restlessness of the mind be conquered?*

Mātājī: By intense love for God.

Question: *We do not want unhappiness and yet it comes. We want real and lasting happiness and it does not come. Why?*

Mātājī: Your desire for true happiness is not intense enough. Take the help of a *guru*.

Question: *What is the greatest sin and the greatest virtue?*

Mātājī: Forgetfulness of God is the greatest sin; His constant remembrance is the greatest virtue.

Question: *Is it right to pray to God for all kinds of things?*

Mātājī: The most excellent prayer is for God Himself.

On another occasion someone asked:

If a householder devotee is in trouble, is it right for him to pray to God for redress?

Mātājī: Various attitudes may be adopted. There are those who have dedicated themselves entirely to God. They say: "My Lord, whatever you may do, howsoever You may keep me, it is all right, for Thy will be done." According to the state of people's minds, their conditions differ. Some are at a stage at which they just cannot help praying. Others, when visited by trials and tribulations feel disappointed with God and drop their religious practices. On the other hand, there are persons who turn to God more eagerly when in sorrow. And some remember Him with greater fervor when they are happy. In all circumstances, He is the great healer. To invoke God is always good. For whatever reason you may pray, with whatever motive—at least start praying to Him! Be it for alleviation of distress or for enlightenment, be it even for wealth and possession. The wise ever live in remembrance of God.

Question: *Is it difficult to know which is the true path?*

Mātājī: If you sit with all doors and windows closed, how can you see the path? Open the door and step out, the path will become visible. Once on the way, you will meet other wayfarers, who will advise and guide you as to the path. Your job is to muster whatever strength you have to get underway—thereafter help is assured.

A young European girl asked:

How can I get rid of this fear?

Mātājī: Fear of what?

Inquirer: *I don't know. Just a terrible fear.*

Mātājī: Are you a Christian?

Inquirer: *Yes.*

[1] Taken from *Life and Teachings of Sri Ma Anandamayi* by Bithika Mukerji (Haridwar: Shree Shree Anandamayee Sangha, 1998) and from *That Compassionate Touch of Ma Anandamayee* by Narayan Chaudhuri (Delhi: Motilal Banarsidass, 1998).

Mātājī: So fill your heart and mind with the presence of Christ in you that there cannot be any room for fear.

A bereaved lady declared:

Mā, I had forgotten about the loss of my daughter while you were here. Now that you are going away, I shall be submerged in sorrow as before.

Mātājī: (Laying her hands upon the lady's heart.) No, it will not overwhelm you again if you think of God and repeat His Holy Name constantly.

To a group of children, Mātājī asked:

Will you have me as a friend?

Children: *Yes.*

Mātājī: Will you then remember this friend's words to you? (The children nod their heads, a little doubtfully.) I shall tell you only five things to remember. One, always speak the truth; two, obey your parents and teachers; three, study as much as is expected of you; four, pray to God every morning that He should make you a good boy or girl, and if during the day you have done something untoward, then at night when going to bed, tell Him you are sorry and you will not let it happen again; five, if the above four are done, then you may be a little naughty if you like! (The children laugh with Mā and repeat the five-point program to learn it by heart.)

A housewife came to Mātājī and declared:

Mā, it is difficult to give myself time for japa *or meditation. No sooner do I sit still, then a dozen things happen which require my attention.*

Mātājī: (Smiling in understanding). Suppose you stand at the seashore wishing to go into the water. Can you wait until all the waves have subsided?

On another occasion someone asked:

How can one sustain the remembrance of God throughout day and night?

Mātājī: By practice. By constant practice, anything, howsoever difficult, can be accomplished. Those who meditate, whether their minds are able to concentrate or not, continue their meditation. Whether you like to do *japa* or not, try to adhere to the practice of it all the same. Make an effort to let your mind be filled with God's name at all times. Be it at home or anywhere else, remember that nothing exists outside God.

A young European lady came to Mātājī and asked:

Shall I ever find peace and happiness?

Mātājī: Peace and happiness are found on the path to God, never in the world, where one gets a little happiness which is invariably followed by it shadow—sorrow.

Inquirer: *(After a long conversation). I shall never forget what you have told me.*

Mātājī: Forget? That is not enough. You must meditate at least for five minutes daily along the lines prescribed by your own religion, and do not forget this friend (pointing to herself)!

On another occasion someone declared:

Mā, I have no spiritual aspirations, I am happy as I am.

Mātāji: That is good; we also are talking of happiness. If you have found the secret of it why do you make this statement? Perhaps there is a touch of doubt somewhere? (Mā smiles and the visitor laughs, acknowledging that it is so). To be with God is true happiness.

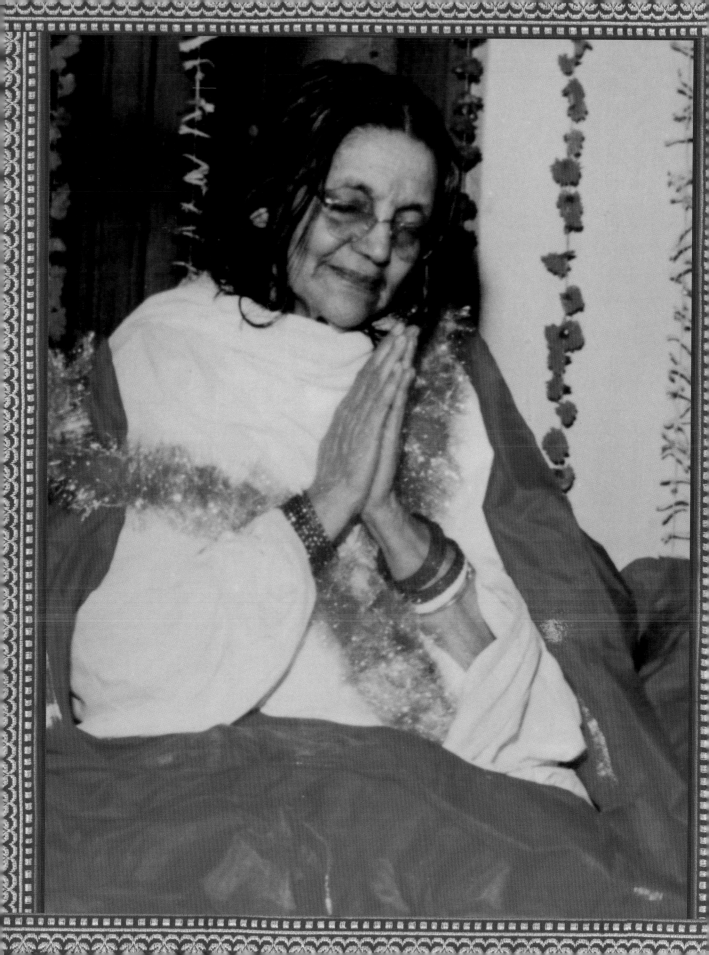

APPENDIX II
A Special Day of Devotion[1]

This daughter of yours implores you all to do one thing, my good fathers and mothers. You are anxious to obtain relief from all the ills you are burdened with. You know when a person is ill he requires both right diet and medicine: your medicine is the repetition of the Divine Name and contemplation of its meaning; your daily diet will be self-control. Practice these two together one special day in the week, or in a fortnight, or at least on one day in the month. The more you can, the better. You should observe the following rules during that special day of devotion:

I. Observe truth in speech, thought, and action.

II. Extreme simplicity in food and dress.

III. Keep the mind serene for that day preferring the eternal to the temporal; with keen devotion dwell constantly on His forms, His messages to man, and His glories as revealed in the *Gītā*.

IV. Try during that day always to bear in mind that God sends all the worries of life for edifying yourself.

V. Keep up a spirit of service for that day believing that your parents, teachers, children, wives, neighbors, are all so many channels through whom your services to them always reach Him.

VI. Ever strengthen the conviction that you are dwelling in Truth, growing in the bosom of the Good and losing yourself to find Him more and more from day to day.

VII. Ever remember that the joys and sorrows of the world are fleeting shadows of your own self; playing with the divine forces brings in everlasting peace and happiness.

VIII. Give your mind a long rope to play with Him; rejoice in the beauties of His forms, attributes, and graces, and in what is stated about Him in the *Śāstra*s or what has been said about Him by the saints of all lands.

IX. When you feel you are not progressing spiritually, always think that you alone are responsible for the setback; fortify your will with more and more strength, with a purer or higher ego-sense, i.e., "I must call out His name," "I will worship Him," "I must learn to love Him." This I-ness pointing to God is better than the self-ego.

X. Remember always during the whole day, repetition of His name has enough power to wash away all sins if there be any, whether of this life or of the past ones.

[1] Taken from Alexander Lipski's *Life and Teaching of Śrī Ānandamayī Mā*.

Glossary of Common Sanskrit Terms

Advaita: Non-dualism. The doctrine that posits the ultimate Reality as one and undifferentiated.

Ajñāna: Ignorance of the true nature of the Self or of Reality. All knowledge other than that of the Self belongs to the category of *ajñāna*. See also *Jñāna*.

Āsana: Yogic posture or physical pose. Every posture corresponds to a particular state of mind. Yogic postures are helpful to concentration. Certain poses are intended also for curative purposes.

Āśram: Hermitage. A place where seekers after Truth live together under the guidance of a *guru*.

Āśrama: Life stage. Successive stages of life, looked at from the viewpoint of a pilgrim on the spiritual path.

Ātmā (Ātman): True Self. Supreme Existence or Being that is of the nature of Self-awareness and Self-delight, and behind all manifestations in nature.

Avatāra: Descent or incarnation of the Divine, usually in one of its aspects or powers.

Bhakta: Devotee. One who advances by the path of *bhakti*.

Bhakti: Devotion and love for God. It is believed that there are mainly three ways of union with God, namely through work done as service (*karma*), through devotion to God (*bhakti*) and through discrimination between the Real and the unreal, which leads to knowledge of the One (*jñāna*). See also *Karma* and *Jñāna*.

Brahmacāri: Religious student who devotes himself to spiritual practices and service and observes strict celibacy.

Brahmacarya: Stage of life of a religious student (*brahmacāri*). See also *Brahmacāri*.

Brāhman: Highest of the four Hindu castes, or a member of that caste.

Brahman: Absolute. Supreme Reality conceived of as one and undifferentiated, static as well as dynamic in character, yet above both.

*Cakra*s: Psychic zones in the human system, which represent the fields of different psychic forces and which have to be conquered, purified, and sublimated by the *yogī* on his upward journey to the sphere of divine consciousness and power.

Darśana: Sight, vision. Having *darśana* of a deity or saint signifies to be blessed by his sight and presence.

Dhyāna: Meditation. Retention of the object of contemplation before the mind's eye. When the stream of attention is broken up (like drops of water), it is called mental concentration; whereas, when the stream is constant (like the flowing of oil), it is called meditation (*dhyāna*). When the distinction between the meditator and the object of meditation ceases to exist, it is called *samādhi*. See also *Samādhi*.

Dīkṣā: Initiation into the spiritual life, given by a spiritual teacher (*guru*) to his disciple (*śiṣya*). During *dīkṣā* the teacher normally imparts to the disciple a particular word of power or name of God (*mantra*). See also *Guru* and *Mantra*.

Durgā: An epithet of Pārvatī, the consort of Śiva.

Dvaitādvaita: The doctrine which holds that ultimate Reality is non-dual and yet dual, looked at from different points of view.

Guru: Spiritual guide and teacher. The candidate for admission into the spiritual life must place himself under the guidance of a competent teacher. During *dīkṣā* (initiation), the *guru* will usually communicate to his new disciple (*śiṣya*) a *mantra* (one of the potent names of God), which must be repeated by the disciple regularly and in a specific manner. See also *Dīkṣā*, and *Mantra*.

Hathayoga: The practice of physical poses (*āsanas*) intended to purify the body and aid in concentration. For Ānandamayī Mā, *hathayoga* is merely a stepping-stone to higher spiritual practices and must not be considered an end in itself.

Iṣṭa: Literally "Beloved." The chosen deity one worships, which appears as a form on the lower plane, but in reality is nothing but the Self that is beyond form.

Jagat: Literally "that which is constantly going," i.e. the world, which is always in a state of change and transition.

Japa: Repetition of a *mantra* (name of God), in a manner specified by a spiritual teacher (*guru*). See also *Guru* and *Mantra*.

Jñāna: Literally "knowledge." True knowledge is of the Self or Reality, every other knowledge, be it through the medium of the senses or the mind, belongs in reality to the category of ignorance (*ajñāna*). See also *Ajñāna*.

Jñāni: One who has attained to true knowledge of the Self or Reality, in other words to enlightenment.

Kālī: Divine Mother in her terrifying aspect.

Karma: Action, the result of action, as well as the law of cause and effect by which actions inevitably bear their fruit. *Karma* originates from the individual self in its ignorance functioning as an active agent. When man realizes his own true Self, *karma* ceases for him.

Karmayoga: Such action as may lead to union with the One; namely work done in a spirit of service, without attachment to the fruit of one's actions.

Kheyāla: Ordinarily a sudden and unexpected psychic emergence, be it desire, will, attention, memory, or knowledge. In Ānandamayī Mā's case a spontaneous manifestation of divine Will.

Kīrtana: Chanting or singing of the names or glories of God, performed by one person or a group of people.

Kṛṣṇa: Eighth incarnation (*avatāra*) of Viṣṇu. See also *Avatāra* and Viṣṇu.

Līlā: Literally "play." Movements and activities of the Supreme Being that are free by nature and not subject to laws. The cosmic show of duality is explained by the *Vaiṣṇava*s as the *līlā* of God.

Mahātmā: Great soul. Used with reference to a person who has destroyed his ego and realized himself as one with the All.

Mahāyoga: Supreme Union; the union of every individual with every other individual, of every object with every other object, and of all individuals and objects with the Universal One.

Mantra: Name of God, or word of power, given to a disciple (*śiṣya*) by a spiritual instructor (*guru*) during initiation (*dīkṣā*). For the *mantra* to be effective, the disciple must practice *japa*, or the regular repetition of the *mantra* in a specified manner. See also *Dīkṣā*, *Guru*, and *Japa*.

Māyā: Illusive power by which the One conceals Itself and appears as the many.

Ojhā: Exorcist of evil spirits.

Pārvatī: Consort of Śiva. See also Śiva.

Prāṇa: The vital energy that functions in various ways in the body for its preservation. Its movement is stimulated and controlled by the practice of *hathayoga*. See also *Hathayoga*.

Praṇām: Obeisance. An act of surrender, indicating the sense of one's own smallness in the presence of the superior.

Pūjā: Ceremonial worship of the Hindus.

Rāma: Seventh incarnation (*avatāra*) of Viṣṇu. See also *Avatāra* and Viṣṇu.

*Ṛṣi*s: Ancient saints or "seers" to whom were revealed the Vedic hymns and *mantra*s. See also *Mantra*.

Śabda Brahman: Literally "Sound *Brahman*." The eternal sound that is the first manifestation of undifferentiated Reality (*Brahman*) and lies at the root of all subsequent creation. See also *Brahman*.

Sadguru: Perfect *guru* who shows the way to the knowledge of Reality.

Sādhanā: Spiritual practice performed for the purpose of preparing oneself for Self-realization.

Sādhikā: One who practices *sādhanā*. See also *Sādhanā*.

Sādhu: One who has dedicated his life to spiritual endeavor.

Śākta: Worshipper of *Śakti*, Divine Energy or the Divine Mother.

Śakti: Divine Energy, usually symbolized as the Divine Mother.

Samādhi: State in which the mind is fused with the object of meditation (*dhyāna*) and becomes luminous, taking on its form; or the mind ceases to function altogether and only pure consciousness remains. See also *Dhyāna*.

Saṁnyāsa: Renunciation. According to Hinduism the last stage of life, when family, possessions, caste, social position, etc. are renounced and man surrenders himself to the Divine.

Saṁnyāsī: One who has taken the vow of renunciation (*saṁnyāsa*). See also *Saṁnyāsa*.

*Samyam Vrata*s: Vow of self-restraint. Practice begun by Ānandamayī Mā in which for one week a year lay devotees abandon worldly living and devote themselves entirely to spiritual pursuits.

*Śāstra*s: The sacred Hindu scriptures.

Satī: Literally "chaste woman." A ritual death wherein a wife burns herself on her husband's funeral pyre as a confirmation of the wife's unconditional loyalty and chastity.

Satsaṅg: Literally "fellowship with truth." The company of saints, sages, and seekers after Truth; a religious meeting.

Śiva: The aspect of the Divine Personality that is associated with the dissolution of the universe; the destroyer of that which is unreal. It can also stand for the Supreme Being Itself.

Tattva: Literally "that-ness" or "essence." The *tattva*s are the primary elements or categories of universal manifestation.

Vairāgya: Detachment from the world and its cause. *Vairāgya* is conceived as a fire, since in that state a burning agony is felt at the least contact with worldly things or sense objects.

Vaiṣṇava: Worshipper of Viṣṇu, the Preserver and Sustainer of the universe, or of one of His incarnations (*avatāra*s). See also Viṣṇu.

Vedas: Sacred scriptures of the Hindus. According to orthodox faith the Vedas are not human compositions, but are supposed to have been directly revealed to the *ṛṣi*s, who were seers, not composers. See also *Ṛṣi*s.

Vedānta: Literally the concluding portion of the Vedas, also known as the Upaniṣads, which represent the philosophical section of Vedic literature. The subject matter of *Vedānta* is knowledge of the Supreme.

*Vibhūti*s: Supernormal powers acquired by a *yogī* in the course of his journey towards perfection. These powers are realized through purification of the mind. Fundamentally all *vibhūti*s are mental powers.

Viṣṇu: Aspect of the Divine Personality that is associated with the preservation of the universe. It can also stand for the Supreme Being Itself.

Yoga: Literally "union." Various methods of achieving the union of the individual self (*jīvātman*) with the universal Self (*Ātman*). See also *Ātmā*.

Yogī: One who practices *yoga* or has mastered it.

Index

Biographical Notes

ALEXANDER LIPSKI was Professor of History and Religious Studies at California State University, Long Beach from 1958 to 1984, and is currently Professor Emeritus. He is the author of *Thomas Merton and Asia: His Quest for Utopia*, and is the editor of *Bengal: East and West*. His book *Life and Teaching of Śrī Ānandamayī Mā* was first published in India where it has been reprinted numerous times; its inclusion as part of the present work marks its first publication in North America.

JOSEPH A. FITZGERALD studied comparative religion at Indiana University, where he also earned a Doctor of Jurisprudence degree. For more than twenty years he has traveled extensively to traditional cultures throughout the world, including South Asia and India. He has previously edited *Honen the Buddhist Saint: Essential Writings and Official Biography*.

Photo Credits

Courtesy of Sadhana Ashram, San Presto di Assisi, Italia: *vi*, 14, 21, 26, 35, 49, 52, 56, 70, 71, 74, 82, 94, 111, 112, 126, 132.

Mina Azizi: 45 top right, 45 bottom; Michael O. Fitzgerald: 44 top, 44 bottom left, 44 bottom right, 59, 64; Richard Lannoy: xi, 22, 31, 32, 33, 41, 73, 102, 103, 108; Barry McDonald: 80; Susana Marín: 28 top, 45 top left, 77, 79 top, 79 bottom left, 79 bottom right, 81 top, 81 bottom; Harry Oldmeadow: 29 top.

All other photographs of Śrī Ānandamayī Mā are courtesy of the Shree Shree Anandamayee Sangha, with thanks to Christopher Pegler for his assistance.

Titles on Hinduism by World Wisdom

Abhishiktananda: A Christian Pilgrim in India,
by Harry Oldmeadow, 2008

The Essential Sri Anandamayi Ma: Life and Teachings of a 20th century Indian Saint,
by Alexander Lipski and Sri Anandamayi Ma, 2007

The Essential Swami Ramdas: Commemorative Edition,
compiled by Susunaga Weeraperuma, 2005

The Essential Vedanta: A New Source Book of Advaita Vedanta,
edited by Eliot Deutsch and Rohit Dalvi, 2004

A Guide to Hindu Spirituality,
by Arvind Sharma, 2006

Introduction to Hindu Dharma,
by the 68th Jagadguru of Kanchi, HH Sri Chandrasekharendra Saraswati Swamigal,
edited by Michael Oren Fitzgerald, 2008

Lamp of Non-Dual Knowledge & Cream of Liberation: Two Jewels of Indian Wisdom,
translated by Swami Sri Ramanananda Saraswathi, 2003

Paths to Transcendence: According to Shankara, Ibn Arabi & Meister Eckhart,
by Reza Shah-Kazemi, 2006

Timeless in Time: Sri Ramana Maharshi,
by A.R. Natarajan, 2006

Tripura Rahasya: The Secret of the Supreme Goddess,
translated by Swami Sri Ramanananda Saraswathi, 2002

Unveiling the Garden of Love: Mystical Symbolism in Layla Majnun & Gitagovinda,
by Lalita Sinha, 2009